T0325252

Mastering NativeScript

Mastering NativeScript helps readers master the NativeScript framework for faster and more robust mobile app development.

Mobile devices have progressed from a mere means of communication to becoming a critical business tool in recent years. People are increasingly glued to their smartphones as technology advances at breakneck speed. The significance of mobile app development cannot be overstated.

And when it comes to mobile app development, NativeScript is a hot topic.

NativeScript was introduced by Telerik, and it allows you to develop truly native apps for iOS and Android under a single code base using JavaScript or TypeScript, XML, and a subset of CSS. The charm of NativeScript is that it enables us to code once for multiple platforms (iOS≤7.1 and Android≤4.1), simultaneously sharing code amongst them while still allowing developers to add platform-specific instructions with flawless execution. As a result, you may release an app for both platforms using a single code base.

NativeScript is comprised of three parts: a JavaScript (JS) virtual machine, a runtime, and a bridge module. The JS virtual machine is used for interpretation and execution of JavaScript code. The bridge module then converts the calls to platform-specific API calls and returns the outcome to the caller.

NativeScript is a very appealing paradigm, and is rising in popularity as we speak. It can be used to construct practically any program, including communication apps (news and social networking), gaming applications (Chess, Tic-tac-toe, pinball), and chat apps. It can also handle maps and geolocation apps.

With *Mastering NativeScript*, learning NativeScript becomes straightforward, which will undoubtedly help readers advance their careers.

The *Mastering Computer Science* series is edited by Sufyan bin Uzayr, a writer and educator with over a decade of experience in the computing field.

Mastering Computer Science
Series Editor: Sufyan bin Uzayr

For more information about this series, please visit: https://www.routledge.com/Mastering-Computer-Science/book-series/MCS

The "Mastering Computer Science" series of books are authored by the Zeba Academy team members, led by Sufyan bin Uzayr.

Zeba Academy is an EdTech venture that develops courses and content for learners primarily in STEM fields, and offers education consulting to Universities and Institutions worldwide. For more info, please visit https://zeba.academy

Mastering NativeScript
A Beginner's Guide

Edited by

Sufyan bin Uzayr

CRC Press
Taylor & Francis Group
Boca Raton London New York

CRC Press is an imprint of the
Taylor & Francis Group, an **informa** business

First Edition published 2023
by CRC Press
6000 Broken Sound Parkway NW, Suite 300, Boca Raton, FL 33487-2742

and by CRC Press
2 Park Square, Milton Park, Abingdon, Oxon, OX14 4RN

CRC Press is an imprint of Taylor & Francis Group, LLC

© 2023 Sufyan bin Uzayr

Library of Congress Cataloging-in-Publication Data

Names: Bin Uzayr, Sufyan, editor.
Title: Mastering NativeScript : a beginner's guide / edited by Sufyan bin Uzayr.
Description: First edition. | Boca Raton : CRC Press, 2023. | Series:
Mastering computer science
Identifiers: LCCN 2022021415 (print) | LCCN 2022021416 (ebook) |
ISBN 9781032289762 (hardback) | ISBN 9781032289731 (paperback) |
ISBN 9781003299394 (ebook)
Subjects: LCSH: NativeScript (Software framework) | JavaScript (Computer
program language) | Software frameworks. | Mobile apps. | Application
software--Development.
Classification: LCC QA76.76.N38 M37 2023 (print) | LCC QA76.76.N38 (ebook) |
DDC 005.2/762--dc23/eng/20220810
LC record available at https://lccn.loc.gov/2022021415
LC ebook record available at https://lccn.loc.gov/2022021416

ISBN: 9781032289762 (hbk)
ISBN: 9781032289731 (pbk)
ISBN: 9781003299394 (ebk)

DOI: 10.1201/9781003299394

Typeset in Minion
by KnowledgeWorks Global Ltd.

Contents

Preface

The *Mastering Computer Science* covers a wide range of topics, spanning programming languages as well as modern-day technologies and frameworks. The series has a special focus on beginner-level content, and is presented in an easy-to-understand manner, comprising:

- Crystal-clear text, spanning various topics sorted by relevance,

- A special focus on practical exercises, with numerous code samples and programs,

- A guided approach to programming, with step-by-step tutorials for the absolute beginners,

- Keen emphasis on real-world utility of skills, thereby cutting the redundant and seldom-used concepts and focusing instead of industry-prevalent coding paradigm, and

- A wide range of references and resources to help both beginner and intermediate-level developers gain the most out of the books.

The *Mastering Computer Science* series of books start from the core concepts, and then quickly move on to industry-standard coding practices, to help learners gain efficient and crucial skills in as little time as possible. The books assume no prior knowledge of coding, so even the absolute newbie coders can benefit from this series.

The *Mastering Computer Science* series is edited by Sufyan bin Uzayr, a writer and educator with more than a decade of experience in the computing field.

About the Author

Sufyan bin Uzayr is a writer, coder, and entrepreneur with over a decade of experience in the industry. He has authored several books in the past, pertaining to a diverse range of topics, ranging from History to Computers/IT.

Sufyan is the Director of Parakozm, a multinational IT company specializing in EdTech solutions. He also runs Zeba Academy, an online learning and teaching vertical with a focus on STEM fields.

Sufyan specializes in a wide variety of technologies such as JavaScript, Dart, WordPress, Drupal, Linux, and Python. He holds multiple degrees, including ones in Management, IT, Literature, and Political Science.

Sufyan is a digital nomad, dividing his time between four countries. He has lived and taught in universities and educational institutions around the globe. Sufyan takes a keen interest in technology, politics, literature, history, and sports, and in his spare time, he enjoys teaching coding and English to young students.

Learn more at sufyanism.com.

CHAPTER 1

The Basics

IN THIS CHAPTER

> ➤ Intro to NativeScript

> ➤ Getting started

> ➤ Anatomy of a NativeScript app

In the early days of mobile applications (pre-iPhone), there was little emphasis on building code once and releasing it to numerous platforms. Developers were only concerned with getting an app into the Apple or Google Play stores as soon as possible. And if it meant that their software wouldn't work on all platforms, it was an acceptable trade-off.

Today, the mobile world is constantly evolving, making it increasingly challenging to stay up with the latest technologies. As developers create apps, they must reach the broadest potential audience: concentrating on a single platform is no longer an option. Apps must be available on several platforms and devices.

To stay up with the ever-changing environment, developers value any technology to streamline the mobile app development process.

Developers now have several options for creating mobile apps targeting numerous platforms from a single code base. NativeScript is one of these options, but it is far from the only one. Others, such as PhoneGap, Xamarin, and React Native, may be familiar to us. Each of these frameworks can create code once and deliver it to both Android and iOS, but we're not here to dispute which framework is superior.

DOI: 10.1201/9781003299394-1

Instead, we want to learn how to create great cross-platform mobile apps utilizing our current abilities. We can develop a mobile app using NativeScript whether we're a newbie who knows the fundamentals of writing web apps with HTML, JavaScript, and CSS or a seasoned professional.

We'll teach how to create cross-platform programs from a single code base utilizing NativeScript's structured approach. When we're completed, we'll be able to construct our own Android and iOS mobile apps using our choice of technologies: HTML, JavaScript, and CSS or Angular, TypeScript, and CSS.

In general, creating a mobile application is a time-consuming and challenging operation. There are several frameworks available for creating a mobile application. Android provides a native framework based on the Java programming language, whereas iOS provides a native framework based on the Objective-C/Shift programming language. However, to create an application that works with both operating systems, we must write in two distinct languages and use two different frameworks.

Mobile frameworks support this functionality to solve this complication. The primary motivation for using a cross-platform or hybrid framework is to maintain a single code base more accessible. NativeScript, Apache Cordova, Xamarin, and more well-known frameworks are included.

JavaScript FRAMEWORK OVERVIEW

JavaScript is a multi-paradigm programming language. It allows for functional, object-oriented, and prototype-based programming. Initially, JavaScript was employed on the client-side. JavaScript is now also employed as a server-side programming language. JavaScript frameworks are tools that make working with JavaScript easier and more fluid.

Using this framework, programmers may quickly create a device-responsive application. One of several factors why this framework is becoming so popular is its responsiveness.

Let's have a look at a few of the most popular JavaScript frameworks.

Angular

Angular is a robust, efficient, and open-source JavaScript framework. We can create both mobile and desktop applications. Google uses this framework. It is used to create a Single Page Application (SPA).

Vue.js

Vue.js is a progressive JavaScript framework for creating dynamic web interfaces. It is a well-known framework for making web development easier. It can be readily integrated into large projects for front-end development. One of the most appealing characteristics for developing high-end SPAs is its dual integration option.

ReactJS

ReactJS is a JavaScript toolkit for creating reusable user interface (UI) components. Facebook created it. It is presently one of the most popular JavaScript libraries with a solid base and a vast community.

Node.js

Node.js is a cross-platform open-source runtime environment for creating server-side and networking applications. It is based on the JavaScript Engine of Google Chrome (V8 Engine). Applications built with Node.js are written in JavaScript and may be executed on OS X, Microsoft Windows, and Linux. It includes an extensive collection of JavaScript modules that simplify the construction of web applications.

NativeScript OVERVIEW

NativeScript is a free and open-source framework for creating native iOS and Android mobile apps. It is a framework that has been just-in-time (JIT)-compiled. NativeScript code is executed on the JavaScript virtual machine. It makes use of the V8 engine runtime on both the Android and iOS platforms. NativeScript is built with XML, JavaScript, and CSS. It features a WebIDE called PlayGround. This PlayGround includes an easy-to-use interface, project management, hot reloading, and device debugging.

NativeScript enables developers to rapidly and effectively construct native, cross-platform programs while saving money on the development, testing, and training. As a result, native applications will continue to be rich and powerful for years to come to make them better and simpler to use.

Furthermore, NativeScript provides a plethora of features that make it simple to get started and use existing skills:

- Uses your existing understanding of HTML, JavaScript, and CSS (no knowledge of Objective C, Swift, or Java is required).
- Your code is only written once.

- Access to Android and iOS native platform APIs.

- An opinionated approach to app development that aids in the organization of our code base.

- Natively integrates with Angular (but is not required to).

Learning a new language can sometimes be a barrier to entering a new world. When developing NativeScript apps, we'll use our prior expertise in HTML applications to swiftly design an app that targets numerous platforms (Android and iOS). Because we already have these abilities, designing NativeScript apps will be a breeze. Plus, we won't have to learn Objective C, Swift, or Java.

HOW ARE NativeScript APPS CREATED?

As shown in the following diagram, NativeScript apps are created in a mix of JavaScript, XML, and CSS.

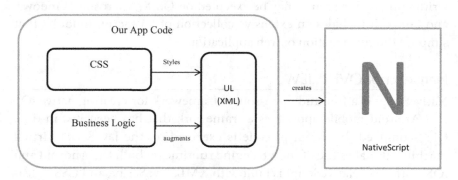

App in NativeScript.

When we build NativeScript apps, our code is divided into three sections: JavaScript, XML, and CSS. The JavaScript component executes business logic, retrieves data, and controls the app's flow. The XML part defines the UI, and CSS is used to customize the UI the same way that an HTML application is.

NativeScript programs have a similar structure and code to HTML apps, but that's where the similarities end. NativeScript is unique in the cross-platform mobile app arena since it allows you to write your UI (XML) code only once.

When the UI code is executed, it renders native UI components in the app. On iOS, for example, UI components are represented as native iOS buttons, dropdowns, and lists. Similarly, UI elements on Android are represented as native Android components.

Other cross-platform frameworks may need to spend time implementing platform-specific view code. The ability to write our UI code once and have it rendered as native UI components, on the other hand, distinguishes NativeScript from other frameworks.

Another distinguishing characteristic of NativeScript is the availability of Native APIs.

As we learn more about NativeScript, we'll see that it runs all of our code as native code on the device. This enables us to benefit from the performance benefits of native code without having to learn or write Objective C, Swift, or Java.

WHAT NativeScript MEANS IN THE CONTEXT OF MOBILE DEVELOPMENT

Consider yourself 15 years ago, when we were lugging around a Windows 6 mobile phone or obsessing over the latest Samsung Blackjack: this was before Android and iOS. There were just fewer platforms and gadgets available back then. New devices are released regularly nowadays. As the volume and diversity of mobile app creation have increased, the development community has begun to explore more effective approaches to design mobile apps that target all platforms.

Various Sorts of Mobile Apps

Mobile apps are classified into four types: native, hybrid, cross-compiled, and JIT-compiled.

Different sorts of mobile apps and the most popular frameworks:

Mobile App Type	Framework
Native	Android, iOS
Hybrid	PhoneGap/Cordova
Cross-compiled	Xamarin
JIT-compiled	NativeScript

With the exception of native applications, the other three app categories in the table share the same goal: create our app code once and publish it across various platforms (which is what people mean when they say cross-platform).

Although the cross-platform frameworks described above achieve comparable aims, they do it in different ways.

WHY IS NativeScript IMPORTANT?

Aside from JIT compilation, NativeScript differs from other mobile app frameworks in several ways. We believe the most significant distinction is our ability to develop completely native apps from a single code base and distribute them unchanged to both Android and iOS.

We've dealt with several mobile app frameworks in the past, and NativeScript stands out in our perspective. We had to build a lot of shim code in other frameworks. This shim code functions similarly to a piece of wood used to level a stove in your kitchen or to assist frame a doorway.

To extend the idea, assume we're putting in a new door and frame. Most doors are made to set width, height, and depth and fit virtually perfectly. However, in all situations, a little shim here and a little shim there is required to get it to fit perfectly. When building code in other frameworks, it's similar: we add a little UI code to make a button seem exactly right on the Android version of the app and a little more UI code to make it appear just right on iOS.

Getting to Market Quickly

So, what does all of this mean? Less shim code, write once, deploy everywhere, and so on. We don't want to squander your time, whether we're a business, an individual developer, or a casual hobbyist. And, because we'll spend less time creating a new app (less shim code, write-one, and deploy everywhere), we'll have more time to innovate and deliver more features in less time.

WHAT KINDS OF APPS MAY BE CREATED WITH NativeScript?

Now that we understand how NativeScript works, we must understand the kind of mobile apps we can create. NativeScript apps, as we may recall, run directly on the device and are interpreted by a JavaScript virtual machine running within the app. This implies that NativeScript apps may access native device APIs and hardware; therefore, any software can be created as a NativeScript app.

Let's start with app kinds that shouldn't be created using NativeScript.

Graphic Intensive Games

To begin with, don't use NativeScript to create graphically heavy games.

Assume we're working on the next great mobile game, Floppy Bunny, which uses a lot of graphical and processing capacity to generate dense

3D visuals. While NativeScript is reasonably performant out of the box, there are probably better platforms designed specifically for producing high-performance 3D games.

After all, NativeScript programs operate within a JavaScript virtual machine, so there is an additional, if minor, layer of abstraction between our app and the raw metal. To get the most out of a gadget and make Floppy Bunny a smashing success, we might consider building a native Android or iOS app.

Line-of-Business and Consumer Apps

Don't be discouraged since we dashed our hopes of authoring Floppy Bunny. NativeScript is also useful for creating various sorts of applications. Unlike our game example, NativeScript is ideal for creating a line-of-business app such as a news feed, companion app for a website, social networking app, or even an app to control all of our home's intelligent gadgets. In reality, there are currently many apps created in NativeScript spanning a wide range of sectors.

FEATURES OF NativeScript

NativeScript has a thriving community behind it. The following are some of NativeScript's standout features:

- Replacement of a Hot Module
- It is simple to set up
- Extensible
- We can create complex animations, graphs, charts, and lists
- Any view may be used as the root of an application by developers
- Coding that is sluggish

BENEFITS OF NativeScript

NativeScript assists small- and large-scale businesses in developing cross-platform mobile apps. Among the many advantages are as follows:

- It is open-source and free. This means we may contribute to the code and use it in any way we choose as long as we don't breach the Apache 2.0 license.

- It enables the creation of genuinely native apps for Android and iOS devices. Each UI component exposed by NativeScript is converted into its equivalent native UI component.

- It allows us to use JavaScript code to access native platform APIs. We don't need to know Java or Objective-C to leverage native platform APIs because we can write everything in JavaScript. This implies that if we need to access a specific device feature, we can learn how to use JavaScript to access native APIs, and we'll be ready to go.

- It provides consumers with a more native-like experience than hybrid mobile app frameworks such as Cordova.

- It enables developers to effortlessly create, deploy, and manage NativeScript apps using the Telerik platform.

- It supports new native platforms with zero-day vulnerabilities. This means we'll be able to access the most recent native APIs and UI components as soon as Google or Apple upgrades their platforms.

- TypeScript may be used to create NativeScript applications. TypeScript is a language that transpiles to JavaScript and extends JavaScript with object-oriented programming features.

- Any JavaScript library that does not rely on the browser or the DOM that you discover on npm may be used within NativeScript. Utility libraries, such as lodash and underscore, are examples of such libraries.

- The NativeScript CLI allows us to accomplish practically anything. The fundamentals are covered by establishing a new project, adding a platform, running on a device, and deploying to a specific platform. In addition, we may install plugins, debug the app, and publish it to the app store.

WORKING WITH NativeScript

Writing native mobile apps with JavaScript, XML, and CSS isn't something we hear about very often. Instead, we've probably heard of developing native mobile apps in Objective C, Swift, or Java. NativeScript enables the creation of native mobile apps through multiple components, including the NativeScript runtime, core modules, JavaScript virtual machines, our app code, and the NativeScript command-line interface (CLI). The following diagram depicts how these components interact to produce native Android and iOS projects, then developed into native programs that run on mobile devices.

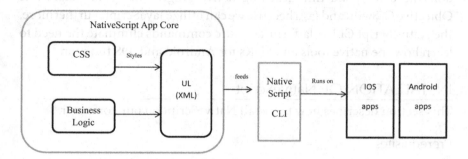

Components of NativeScript.

We already know: the code for our app is written in JavaScript, CSS, and XML. After we've developed our code, it will communicate with the NativeScript runtime and code modules. Finally, the NativeScript CLI tool combines your code, the NativeScript runtime, and NativeScript core modules into a native program that includes a JavaScript virtual machine. This native app is then available for both Android and iOS.

Taking a Deeper Dive

After constructing our UI with XML, we style the UI with CSS (like CSS is used to style HTML apps). Then we create JavaScript to enhance our UI. Writing business logic that responds to events (such as the app launch event) and interactions will be part of our JavaScript code (like a button tap or finger swipe). These three components (UI written in XML, CSS, and business logic written in JavaScript) work together to form our app code.

Our app code does not have all it needs to function on a mobile device on its own; it also requires the assistance of three extra components: the NativeScript runtime, core modules, and a JavaScript virtual engine. Remember that our app code and these three components constitute the foundation of our NativeScript program.

After we've finished developing our program, it's fed into the NativeScript CLI. The CLI is in charge of developing native Android and iOS projects and integrating the NativeScript app core into each project. When Executed, the CLI invokes the native Android or iOS software development kits (SDKs) to create and assemble a native app. Subsequently, the built program is deployed (through the command line interface) and runs on a physical device, simulator, or emulator.

As we can see, the appeal of NativeScript resides in its universality: we don't need to spend time learning native programming languages like Objective C, Swift, and Java because we can utilize JavaScript. Furthermore, the NativeScript CLI's platform-agnostic commands eliminate the need to learn how the native tools and SDKs for Android and iOS function.

INSTALLATION OF NativeScript

This section describes how to install NativeScript on our computer.

Prerequisites

Before proceeding with installation, the following conditions must be met:

- Node.js

- iOS

- Android

Verify Node.js

Node.js is a JavaScript runtime engine built on top of Google Chrome's internal JavaScript engine, v8. NativeScript actively employs Node.js for various purposes, such as developing the initial template application, compiling the application, etc. Node.js must be installed on your PC.

Hopefully, we have Node.js installed on your PC. If it isn't already installed, go to https://nodejs.org/ and download and install the newest LTS package.

To see if Node.js is correctly installed, run the following command in our terminal:

```
node -version
```

CLI Setup

NativeScript CLI is a command-line program that allows us to construct and develop NativeScript applications. NativeScript CLI is installed on our PC via the Node.js package manager npm.

To install NativeScript CLI, run the following command:

```
npm install -g nativescript
```

setupcli

We have the most recent NativeScript CLI, tns, installed on our machine. Now, on our terminal, enter the following command:

tns

cli

Even without any further configuration, we can utilize tns to construct and develop applications. However, we were unable to install the program on a real device. Instead, we may use the NativeScript PlayGround iOS/Android app to launch the program.

Installing the NativeScript Playground Application

Navigate to the iOS App Store or Google Play Store and look for the NativeScript Playground app. When the program appears in the search results, click the install button. It will download and install the NativeScript Playground software into our smartphone.

The NativeScript Playground application will allow you to test your apps on Android or iOS devices without deploying them to a real device or emulator. This would shorten the time required to construct the application and provide an easier approach to getting started with creating our mobile application.

Configuration for Android and iOS

In this section, we will learn how to configure the system to write and execute iOS and Android apps in an emulator or on a real device.

- **Step 1: Dependency of Windows:** Run the following command as an administrator at our Windows command prompt.

```
@powershell -NoProfile -ExecutionPolicy Bypass
-Command "iex
((new-object net.webclient).DownloadString
('https://www.nativescript.org/setup/win'))"
```

Following this command, the scripts are downloaded, and the dependencies are installed and configured.

- **Step 2: Dependency of macOS:** To install in macOS, we must first check to see if Xcode is installed. NativeScript requires the use of Xcode. If Xcode is not already installed, go to https://developer.apple .com/xcode/ and download; then install it.

Now, on the terminal, type the following command:

```
sudo ruby -e "$(curl -fsSL https://www
.nativescript.org/setup/mac)"
```

Following the above command's execution, the script will install the necessary for both iOS and Android development. When it's finished, shut and restart the terminal.

- **Step 3: Dependency of Android:** Hopefully, we've set up the necessary prerequisites:

  - JDK 8 or higher

  - Android Support Repository

  - Google Repository

  - Android Studio

  - Android SDK

  - Android SDK Build-tools 28.0.3 or higher

If the prerequisites listed above are not met, go to https://developer.android.com/studio/ and install it. Finally, add the environment variables JAVA HOME and ANDROID HOME.

- **Step 4: Confirm dependencies:** Everything is now completed. We can test the dependence using the following command:

  ```
  tns doctor
  ```

ARCHITECTURE IN NativeScript

NativeScript is a sophisticated framework for developing mobile applications. It conceals the complexities of developing mobile applications and provides a straightforward API for developing highly efficient and powerful mobile applications. NativeScript allows even inexperienced developers to create mobile applications for both Android and iOS.

Let's have a look at the NativeScript framework's architecture.

The NativeScript framework's fundamental notion is to allow developers to construct hybrid-style mobile applications. A hybrid application hosts a web application within a standard mobile application using the platform-specific browser API and offers system access to the application via the JavaScript API.

NativeScript places a high value on the JavaScript programming language to create an efficient environment for developers. Because JavaScript is the de-facto standard for client-side programming (Web development) and every developer is familiar with the JavaScript language, it makes it easier for developers to get started with the NativeScript framework. NativeScript provides the native API at the lowest level via a set of JavaScript plugins known as Native plugins.

NativeScript expands based on Native plugins by providing a plethora of high-level and simple-to-use JavaScript modules. Each module performs a specific job, such as accessing a camera or constructing a screen. All of these modules may be integrated with a variety of ways to create a complicated mobile application.

Overview of the NativeScript Framework at a High Level

- **NativeScript application:** NativeScript framework enables developers to use either an Angular or a Vue style application.

- **JavaScript modules:** The NativeScript framework has many JavaScript modules explicitly labeled as UI modules, Application modules, Core modules, and so on. All modules may be accessible at any moment by the program, allowing it to create any degree of complicated application.

- **JavaScript plugins:** NativeScript framework has a vast array of JavaScript plugins for accessing platform-related functions. Modules use JavaScript plugins to offer platform-specific functionality.

- **Native plugins:** Native plugins are built in a platform-specific language to cover the system functionality utilized by the JavaScript plugin.

- **Platform API:** APIs given by platform manufacturers are referred to as platform APIs.

In a nutshell, modules are used to construct and organize NativeScript applications. Modules are written in pure JavaScript, and modules access platform-related functionality via plugins, which, in turn, bridge the platform API and JavaScript API.

A NativeScript APPLICATION'S WORKFLOW

NativeScript applications are made up of modules. Each module allows a different functionality. The following are the two most critical types of modules for bootstrapping a NativeScript application:

- Page modules

- Root modules

Application modules include the Root and Page modules. The application module serves as the NativeScript application's entry point. It bootstraps a page, allowing the developer to design the page's UI, and lastly, allows the page's business logic to be executed. An application module is made up of the three things listed below:

- XML-based UI design (e.g., page.xml/page.component.html)

- CSS-coded styles (e.g., page.css/page.component.css)

- Actual module business logic in JavaScript (e.g., page.js/page.component.ts)

NativeScript has a plethora of UI components for designing the application page. In an Angular-based application, UI components can be expressed in XML or HTML format. The application module uses the UI component to create the page, saved in a separate XML file, page.xml/page.component.html. CSS may be used to style the design.

The design style is stored in a different CSS file, page.css/page.component.css, in application modules. The page's functionality may be implemented using JavaScript/TypeScript, which has full access to the design and platform functionalities. The actual functionality of the page is coded in a different file, page.js/page.component.ts, by the application module.

Root Modules

NativeScript uses UI containers to control the UI and user interaction. Every UI container should have a root module via which it maintains its UI. There are two types of UI containers in NativeScript applications:

- **Application container:** Each NativeScript application should have one application container, which is configured using the application. run() function. It sets up the application's UI.

- **Mobile view container:** NativeScript manages Modal dialogues with the help of a model view container. Any number of model view containers can be used in a NativeScript application.

Like its content, each root module should only have one UI component. The UI component, in turn, might have children that are other UI components. NativeScript has many UI components with child functionality, such as TabView, ScrollView, and others. These can be used as the primary UI component. The frame is an exception since it does not have a child option but may be used as the root component. The frame has options for loading Page modules as well as navigating to other Page modules.

Page Modules

Every page in NativeScript is essentially a Page module. The Page module is built with NativeScript's extensive range of UI components. Page modules are loaded into the application via the Frame component (by its defaultPage attribute or the navigate() function), which is then loaded via Root modules, which is then loaded via the application. While the program is running, use run().

ANGULAR-BASED NativeScript APPLICATION WORKFLOW

As previously said, the NativeScript framework offers a variety of approaches to appeal to various types of developers. NativeScript supports the following methodologies:

- NativeScript Core is the foundational notion of the NativeScript Framework.

- Angular + NativeScript methodology based on Angular.

- Vuejs + NativeScript methodology based on Vue.js.

Let's have a look at how the Angular framework is integrated into the NativeScript framework.

- **Step 1:** To bootstrap the Angular application, NativeScript offers an object (platformNativeScriptDynamic). The bootstrapModule function of platformNativeScriptDynamic is used to start the program.

The following is the syntax for bootstrapping the application with the Angular framework:

```
import { platformNativeScriptDynamic } from
"nativescript-angular/platform";
import { AppModule } from "./app/app.module";
platformNativeScriptDynamic().bootstrapModule
(AppModule);
```

- **Step 2:** A basic implementation of the app module:

```
import { NgModule } from "@angular/core";
import { NativeScriptModule } from "nativescript-
angular/nativescript.module";
import { AppRoutingModule } from "./app-routing
.module";
import { AppComponent } from "./app.component";
@NgModule(
    {
        bootstrap: [
        AppComponent
    ], imports: [
        NativeScriptModule,
        AppRoutingModule
    ], declarations: [
        AppComponent
    ]
    }
) export class AppModule { }
```

AppModule loads the AppComponent component to begin the application. Angular components are similar to pages in that they are utilized for design as well as programming functionality.

The following is a small implementation of AppComponent (app. component.ts) and its display logic (app.component.css):

- **app.component.ts:**

```
import { Component } from "@angular/core";
@Component(
    {
        selector: "ns-app",
        templateUrl: "app.component.html"
    }
)
export class AppComponent { }
```

- **app.component.html:**

```
<page-router-outlet></page-router-outlet>
```

The Angular application is linked to the page-router-outlet.

In summary, the Angular framework comprises modules that are comparable to those found in the NativeScript framework but differ somewhat. Each Angular module will contain an Angular component and a router setup file (page-routing.mocdule.ts). The router is configured per module and handles navigation. Pages in NativeSctipt core are analogous to Angular components.

Each component will have a UI design (page.component.html), a style sheet (page.component.css), and a JavaScript/TypeScript code file (page.component.ts).

ANGULAR APPLICATION IN NativeScript

To understand the workflow of the NativeScript application, let us build a small, bare-bones application.

Developing the Application

Let's look at how to make a small application with NativeScript CLI, tns. To start a new project with NativeScript, use the tns command create.

The following is the fundamental syntax for creating a new application:

```
tns create <projectname> --template <template_name>
```

where,

- The project's name is projectname.
- Template name refers to the Project template. NativeScript has a plethora of starter templates for building various types of applications. Make use of an Angular-based template.

To begin on our new program, let us establish a new directory called NativeScriptSamples. Now, start a new terminal, navigate to our directory, and enter the following command:

```
tns create BlankNgApp --template tns-template-blank-ng
```

Whereas tns-template-blank-ng refers to a blank AngularJS mobile application.

Application Architecture

Let's learn about the structure of a NativeScript application by examining our first program in this chapter, BlankNgApp. The NativeScript program is divided into several sections, which are as follows:

- Section on configuration

- Modules for nodes

- Sources for Android

- Sources for iOS

- Source code for an application.

The application's general structure is as follows:

```
| angular.json
| LICENSE
| nsconfig.json
| package-lock.json
| package.json
| tsconfig.json
| tsconfig.tns.json
| tsfmt.json
| webpack.config.js
|
├────App_Resources
|    ├────Android
|    |
|    └────iOS
|
├────hooks
|
├────node_modules
|
└────src
     | app.css
     | main.ts
     | package.json
     |
     └────app
```

```
|    app-routing.module.ts
|    app.component.html
|    app.component.ts
|    app.module.ts
|
└────home
     home-routing.module.ts
     home.component.html
     home.component.ts
     home.module.ts
```

Let us examine each element of the application and how it contributes to the development of our application.

Configuration

All of the files in the application's root directory are configuration files. The configuration files are in JSON format, making it easier for the developer to comprehend the setup specifics. The NativeScript program relies on these files to obtain all configuration information. In this part, we'll go through all of the configuration files.

- **package.json:** package.json files set the identity (id) of the application and all the modules that the application depends on for its proper working. Below is our package.json:

```
{
    "nativescript": {
        "id": "org.nativescript.BlankNgApp",
        "tns-android": {
            "version": "6.3.1"
        }, "tns-ios": {
            "version": "6.3.0"
        }
    }, "description": "NativeScript Application",
    "license": "SEE LICENSE IN
<your-license-filename>",
    "repository": "<fill-your-repository-here>",
    "dependencies": {
        "@angular/animations": "~8.2.0",
        "@angular/common": "~8.2.0",
        "@angular/compiler": "~8.2.0",
        "@angular/core": "~8.2.0",
        "@angular/forms": "~8.2.0",
```

```
      "@angular/platform-browser": "~8.2.0",
      "@angular/platform-browser-dynamic":
"~8.2.0",
      "@angular/router": "~8.2.0",
      "@nativescript/theme": "~2.2.1",
      "nativescript-angular": "~8.20.3",
      "reflect-metadata": "~0.1.12",
      "rxjs": "^6.4.0",
      "tns-core-modules": "~6.3.0",
      "zone.js": "~0.9.1"
    },
    "devDependencies": {
      "@angular/compiler-cli": "~8.2.0",
      "@ngtools/webpack": "~8.2.0",
      "nativescript-dev-webpack": "~1.4.0",
      "typescript": "~3.5.3"
    },
    "gitHead":
"fa98f785df3fba482e5e2a0c76f4be1fa6dc7a14",
    "readme": "NativeScript Application"
}
```

Here,

- **Application identity (nativescript/id):** It sets the application's id to org.nativescript.BlankNgApp. This id will be used when we upload our software to the Play Store or iTunes. This identifier will serve as our Application Identifier or Package Name.

- **Dependencies:** Specifies all of our dependent node modules. Angular modules are included since the default NativeScript implementation is based on Angular framework.

- **Development dependencies:** Specifies all of the tools on which the program is dependent. Because we are constructing our application in TypeScript, typescript is included as one of the dependent modules.

- **angular.json:** angular.json contains configuration information for the Angular framework.

- **nsconfig.json:** NativeScript framework configuration data is stored in nsconfig.json.

- **tsconfig.json, tsfmt.json, and tsconfig.tns.json:** TypeScript language configuration information may be found in tsconfig.json, tsfmt.json, and tsconfig.tns.json.

- **webpack.config.js:** webpack.config.js JavaScript configuration for WebPack.

Modules of Node

Because NativeScript is a node-based project, all of its dependencies are stored in the node_modules folder. To download and install all application dependencies into the node_moduels, we may use npm (npm install) or tns.

Source Code of Android

NativeScript produces the android source code and saves it in the App_Resources\Android folder. It will be used to construct an Android app using the Android SDK.

Source Code of iOS

NativeScript produces the iOS source code and saves it in the App_Resources\iOS folder. It will be used to develop iOS applications with the iOS SDK and XCode.

The Application's Source Code

The application code is stored in the src folder. In the src folder of our program, we will find the files listed below:

```
└──src
 |  app.css
 |  main.ts
 |  package.json
 |
 └──app
 |  app-routing.module.ts
 |  app.component.html
 |  app.component.ts
 |  app.module.ts
 |
 └──home
```

```
home-routing.module.ts
home.component.html
home.component.ts
home.module.ts
```

Let us first understand the function of all files in this part and how they are organized.

- **Step 1: main.ts – The application's entry point.**

```
// This import should be performed initially in
order to load certain necessary parameters (like
globals and reflect-metadata)
import { platformNativeScriptDynamic } from
"nativescript-angular/platform";
import { AppModule } from "./app/app.module";
platformNativeScriptDynamic()
.bootstrapModule(AppModule);
```

The AppModule has been designated as the application's bootstrapping module in this case.

- **Step 2: app.css – The application's main style sheet is displayed here.**

```
@import "~@nativescript/theme/css/core.css";
@import "~@nativescript/theme/css/brown.css";
/* Put any CSS rules that wish to apply to both
iOS and Android in this section.
This is where the vast majority of CSS code will
be placed.*/
```

Here,

The NativeScript framework's core style sheet and brown color themes style sheet are imported by app.css.

- **Step 3: app\app.module.ts – The application's root module.**

```
import { NgModule, NO_ERRORS_SCHEMA } from "@
angular/core";
import { NativeScriptModule } from "nativescript-
angular/nativescript.module";
import { AppRoutingModule } from "./app-routing.
module";
import { AppComponent } from "./app.component";
@NgModule(
```

```
{
    bootstrap: [
        AppComponent
    ],
    imports: [
        NativeScriptModule,
        AppRoutingModule
    ],
    declarations: [
        AppComponent
    ], schemas: [
        NO_ERRORS_SCHEMA
    ]
}
)
export class AppModule { }
```

Here,

AppModule is built on NgModule and configures the application's components and modules. It includes two modules, NativeScriptModule and AppRoutingModule, as well as a component, AppComponent. It also made the AppComponent the application's root component.

- **Step 4: app.component.ts – The application's root component.**

```
import { Component } from "@angular/core";
@Component(
    {
        selector: "ns-app",
        templateUrl: "app.component.html"
    }
)
export class AppComponent { }
```

Here,

AppComponent defines the component's template and style sheet. The template is written in plain HMTL and employs NativeScript UI components.

- **Step 5: app-routing.module.ts – AppModule routing module.**

```
import { NgModule } from "@angular/core";
import { Routes } from "@angular/router";
```

```
import { NativeScriptRouterModule } from
"nativescript-angular/router";
const routes: Routes = [
    { path: "", redirectTo: "/home", pathMatch:
"full" },
    { path: "home", loadChildren: () =>
    import("~/app/home/home.module").then((m) =>
m.HomeModule) }
];
@NgModule(
    {
        imports: [NativeScriptRouterModule.
forRoot(routes)],
        exports: [NativeScriptRouterModule]
    }
)
export class AppRoutingModule { }
```

Here,

AppRoutingModule utilizes the NativeScriptRouterModule to configure the AppModule's routes. It essentially redirects the empty route to/home and refers/home to HomeModule.

- **Step 6: app\home\home.module.ts – Creates a new module called HomeModule.**

```
import { NgModule, NO_ERRORS_SCHEMA } from
"@angular/core";
import { NativeScriptCommonModule } from
"nativescript-angular/common";
import { HomeRoutingModule } from "./home-routing.
module";
import { HomeComponent } from "./home.component";
@NgModule(
    {
        imports: [
            NativeScriptCommonModule,
            HomeRoutingModule
        ],
        declarations: [
            HomeComponent
        ],
        schemas: [
            NO_ERRORS_SCHEMA
```

```
        ]
    }
)
export class HomeModule { }
```

Here,

HomeModule imports two modules, HomeRoutingModule and NativeScriptCommonModule, as well as one component, HomeComponent.

- **Step 7: app\home\home.component.ts – Defines the Home component used as the application's home page.**

```
import { Component, OnInit } from "@angular/core";
@Component(
    {
        selector: "Home", templateUrl: "./home.
component.html"
    }
)
export class HomeComponent implements OnInit {
    constructor() {
        // Use the component constructor to inject
providers.
    }
    ngOnInit(): void {
        // Init your component properties here.
    }
}
```

Here,

HomeComponent configures the home component's template and selector.

- **Step 8: app\home\home-routing.module.ts – HomeModule routing module, used to specify routing for the home module.**

```
import { NgModule } from "@angular/core";
import { Routes } from "@angular/router";
import { NativeScriptRouterModule } from
"nativescript-angular/router";
import { HomeComponent } from "./home.component";
const routes: Routes = [
    { path: "", component: HomeComponent }
];
```

```
@NgModule(
    {
        imports: [NativeScriptRouterModule.
forChild(routes)],
        exports: [NativeScriptRouterModule]
    }
)
export class HomeRoutingModule { }
```

Here,

The empty path was set to HomeComponent by HomeRoutingModule.

- **Step 9:** app.component.html and home.component.html – These files are used to construct the application's UI with NativeScript UI components.

Run Our App

If we wish to execute your program without utilizing a device, use the command below:

```
tns preview
```

After running this command, a QR code will be generated to scan and link with our smartphone.

Run Our App on Our Device

If we wish to test the connected device in our application, use the following syntax:

```
'tns device <Platform> --available-devices'
```

After that, we may run our program with the following command:

```
tns run
```

The program above is used to develop your apps locally and then install them on Android or iOS devices. If we wish to execute our program on an Android simulator, use the command below:

```
tns run android
```

We can use the following command on an iOS device:

```
run ios
```

TEMPLATES FOR NativeScript

NativeScript has many ready-made templates for everything from a simple blank but completely functioning application to a complicated Tab-based application.

Using a Template

A new application may be built by using the create subcommand of the tns command:

```
tns create <app-name> --template <tns-template-name>
```

Here,

The template's name is tns-template-name in this case.

If we wish to use JavaScript to generate a template with only one page and no custom styles, use the following command:

```
tns create <app-name> --template tns-template-blank
```

TypeScript may be used to construct the same template as seen above:

```
tns create <app-name> --template tns-template-blank-ts
```

Template for Navigation

The navigation template is used to construct applications ranging from modest to complicate. It includes a pre-configured SideDrawer component with several pages. The SideDrawer component provides a hidden view for navigation UI or common settings. To develop a navigation-based application, use the command below:

```
tns create <app-name> --template tns-template-drawer-
navigation
```

Template for Tab Navigation

To construct a tab-based application, a tab navigation template is utilized. It includes a pre-configured TabView component with several pages. To construct a tab-based application, use the following command:

```
tns create <app-name> --template tns-template-tab-
navigation
```

Template for Master-Detail

The Master-Detail template is used to develop a list-based application that includes a detail page for each item in the list:

```
tns create <app-name> --template tns-template-master-
detail
```

Customized Template

To make a basic customized template, we must first clone blank templates. NativeScript, as you may know, supports JavaScript, TypeScript, Angular, and Vue.js templates, allowing us to select any language and design your own.

For example, use the following command to clone a customized and straightforward template from a git repository.

```
git clone https://github.com/NativeScript/template-
blank-ts.git
```

It will now generate the mobile app framework, allowing you to make adjustments and run your Android/iOS device. This structure is built on a set of rules. Let's take a quick look at the guidelines.

Structure

Our modified template must meet the following conditions:

- Do not put our code in the root folder of our app.

- Make a new folder and place the feature area inside.

- The page, view models, and service should all be placed in the feature section. This aids in the creation of excellent and clear code.

- Create a page folder and place.ts,.xml,.scss/css, and other files within.

package.json: Place the package.json file in the app template's root folder. Use the format to provide a value for the name property.

```
{
    "name": "tns-template-blank-ts",
    displayName": "template-blank",
}
```

Give the version attribute a value. It is defined further down.

```
"version": "3.2.1",
```

Assign a value to the main property that specifies our app's principal entry point. It is defined further down:

```
"main": "app.js",
```

Give the android property a value. It is defined further down:

```
"android": {
    "v8Flags": "--expose_gc"
},
```

The repository attribute should be defined as follows in our code:

```
"repository": {
    "type": "git",
    "url": "https://github.com/NativeScript/
template-master-detail-ts"
},
```

Style: Use the syntax below to import styles and themes into our app template:

```
@import '~nativescript-theme-core/scss/light';
```

We may also use the code below to set a custom background color:

```
/* Color */
$background: #fff;
$primary: lighten(#000, 13%);
```

WIDGETS IN NativeScript

NativeScript has many UI components known as "widgets." Each widget performs a specific function and has a set of methods. In this part, we'll go over NativeScript widgets in depth.

Button

A button is a component that is used to carry out the tap event action. When a user taps the button, the relevant actions are carried out. It is defined further down.

```
<Button text="Click-here" tap="onTap"></Button>
```

Let's add the button to our BlankNgApp as seen below.

- **Step 1:** Navigate to src\app\home\home.component.html. This is the home component's UI design page.

- **Step 2:** Insert a button into the GirdLayout component. The full code is as follows:

```
<ActionBar>
   <Label text="Home"></Label>
</ActionBar>
<GridLayout>
   <button text="Click-Here"></button>
</GridLayout>
```

- **Step 3:** We may style the button with CSS, as seen below:

```
<ActionBar>
   <Label text="Home"></Label>
</ActionBar>
<GridLayout>
   <button text="Click-Here" class="-primary">
</button>
</GridLayout>
```

The -primary class is used to represent the primary button in this case.

- **Step 4:**

```
<GridLayout>
   <Button class="-primary">
      <FormattedString>
         <Span text="&#xf099;" class="fa"></Span>
         <Span text=" Button.-primary with icon ">
</Span>
      </FormattedString>
   </Button>
</GridLayout>
```

```
.fa {
    font-family: "FontAwesome",
"fontawesome-webfont";
}
```

Here,

&#xf099 specifies the position of the icon in the FontAwesome font. Download the most recent Font Awesome font and save fontawesome-webfont.ttf in the src\fonts folder.

- **Step 5:**

```
<Button text="Button.-primary.-rounded-sm"
class="-primary -rounded-sm"></Button>
```

Label

Static text is shown using the Label component. Change the home page to the one shown below:

```
<GridLayout>
    <Label text="NativeScript is an open source
framework for creating native apps in JavaScript or
TypeScript. There are several frameworks available for
creating a mobile application." textWrap="true">
    </Label>
</GridLayout>
```

TextField

The TextField component is used to collect data from the user. Let us modify our home page to the one listed below:

```
<GridLayout>
    <TextField hint="User-name"
        color="lightblue"
        backgroundColor="yellow"
        height="65px">
    </TextField>
</GridLayout>
```

Here,

Color represents the color of the text.

backgroundColor is the color of the text box's background.

The height of the text box is represented by height.

TextView

The TextView Component is used to receive multiline text information from the user. Let us modify our home page to the one listed below:

```
<GridLayout>
    <TextView loaded="onTextViewLoaded" hint="Enter
text" returnKeyType="done" autocorrect="false"
maxLength="90">
    </TextView>
</GridLayout>
```

SearchBar

This component is used to search for and submit queries. It is defined further down:

```
<StackLayout>
    <SearchBar id="bar" hint="click-here to
search.."></SearchBar>
<StackLayout>
```

We can use styles:

```
<StackLayout>
    <SearchBar id="bar" hint="click-here to search.."
color="green" backgroundColor="green"></SearchBar>
</StackLayout>
```

Switch

To choose between choices, switch is based on a toggle. The default value is false. It is defined further down:

```
<StackLayout>
    <Switch checked="false" loaded="onSwitchLoaded">
</Switch>
</StackLayout>
```

Slider

A slider is a sliding component used to choose a numerical range. It is defined further down:

```
<Slider value="25" minValue="0" maxValue="55"
loaded="onSliderLoaded"></Slider>
```

Progress

The Progress widget displays the status of an operation. The current state is indicated by a bar. It is defined further down:

```
<StackLayout verticalAlign="center" height="50">
    <Progress value="85" maxValue="110"
backgroundColor="yellow" color="green" row="0">
</Progress>
</StackLayout>
```

ActivityIndicator

The ActivityIndicator displays a task that is in process. It is defined further down:

```
<StackLayout verticalAlign="center" height="40">
    <ActivityIndicator busy="true" color="blue"
width="50"
    height="40"></ActivityIndicator>
</StackLayout>
```

Image

To show a picture, an image widget is utilized. It may be accessed using the "ImageSource" URI. It is defined further down:

```
<StackLayout class="m-15"
backgroundColor="lightyellow">
    <Image src="~/images/logo1.png"
stretch="aspectFill"></Image>
</StackLayout>
```

WebView

WebView displays web pages. URLs may be used to load web pages. It is defined further down:

```
<WebView row="1" loaded="onWebViewLoaded"
id="myWebView" src="http://www.facebook.com">
</WebView>
```

DatePicker

DatePicker is used to select a date. It is defined further down:

```
<StackLayout class="m-15" backgroundColor="lightgray">
```

```
    <DatePicker year="1980" month="4" day="20"
verticalAlignment="center"></DatePicker>
</StackLayout>
```

TimePicker

The TimePicker component is used to select a time. It is defined further down:

```
<StackLayout class="m-15" backgroundColor="lightgray">
<TimePicker hour="8"
    minute="28"
    maxHour="23"
    maxMinute="59"
    minuteInterval="5">
</TimePicker>
</StackLayout>
```

LAYOUT CONTAINERS IN NativeScript

NativeScript provides a container component collection for the primary purpose of setting up UI widget components. Layout containers perform as the parent component and can have one or more child components. A layout container's child components can all be organized using the approach offered by its parent layout container.

NativeScript has six layout containers, which are as follows:

- Container for absolute layout

- Container for dock arrangement

- Container for grid layout

- Container for stack arrangement

- Wrap layout container

- FlexibleBox is a layout container

In this session, we'll go over all of the layout container principles in depth.

AbsoluteLayout

The AbsoluteLayout container is NativeScript's most basic layout container. AbsoluteLayout imposes no constraints on its children and will position them inside it using a two-dimensional coordinate system with the top-left corner as the origin.

AbsoluteLayout positions its children using four attributes, which are as follows:

- **top:** Defines the child's position in the y direction, starting at the origin and progressing downward.

- **left:** The child is placed to the left of the origin, traveling sideways in the x direction.

- **width:** Defines the child's width.

- **height:** Defines the child's height.

Let us add the AbsoluteLayout container to our application's main page as shown below:

```
<ActionBar>
    <Label text="Home"></Label>
</ActionBar>
<AbsoluteLayout width="210" height="310"
backgroundColor="blue">
    <Label text="Top Left" left="0" top="0" width="110"
height="140" backgroundColor="green">
    </Label>
    <Label text="Top Right" left="100" top="0"
width="110" height="140" backgroundColor="blue">
</Label>
    <Label text="Bottom Left" left="0" top="140"
width="110" height="140" backgroundColor="orange">
    </Label>
    <Label text="Bottom Right" left="110" top="140"
width="110" height="140" backgroundColor="red">
</Label>
</AbsoluteLayout>
```

DockLayout

The DockLayout container component allows its children to dock within it. A child component can dock on each side of the container (top, bottom, left, and right). The DockLayout container docks its children appropriately by using their dock property.

The dock property can have the following values:

- **top:** Dock the child component at the top corner of the layout container.

- **bottom:** Dock the child component at the bottom corner of the Layout container.

- **left:** Dock the child component in the left corner of the Layout container.

- **right:** Dock the child component in the right corner of the Layout container.

DockLayout containers dock their final child component by default. It can override this behavior by setting the stretchLastChild parameter to zero.

Let us add the DockLayout container to our application's main page as seen below:

```
<ActionBar>
    <Label text="Home"></Label>
</ActionBar>
<DockLayout width="240" height="310"
backgroundColor="blue" stretchLastChild="false">
    <Label text="left" dock="left" width="60"
backgroundColor="green"></Label>
    <Label text="top" dock="top" height="60"
backgroundColor="orange"></Label>
    <Label text="right" dock="right" width="60"
backgroundColor="red"></Label<
    <Label text="bottom" dock="bottom" height="60"
    backgroundColor="orange"></Label>
</DockLayout>
```

GridLayout

GridLayout is a complicated layout container that arranges child items in a tabular form with rows and columns. It has one row and one column by default. It has the following characteristics:

1. **columns:** Used to denote the default width of each column, separated by a comma. There are three potential values: number, *, and auto keyword.

where,

- the number represents the absolute column width.

- specifies a column's width concerning other columns. A number can follow it to specify how many times the column width should be relative to the other column. For example, 2* indicates that the column's width should be twice the width of the smallest column.

- auto specifies that the width of the column is the same as the width of its widest child.

For example, *, 2* denotes two columns, the second of which will be double the size of the first.

2. **rows:** Used to denote the default height of each row, separated by a comma. Columns are used to represent values.

GridLayout layouts its children using the attributes listed below:

- **row:** The row number.

- **col:** The number of the column.

- **rowSpan:** rowSpan is the total number of rows that a layout's child content spans.

- **colSpan:** colSpan is the total number of columns that a layout's child content spans.

Let us add the GridLayout container to our application's main page as seen below:

```
<ActionBar>
    <Label text="Home"></Label>
</ActionBar>
<GridLayout columns="40, auto, *" rows="40, auto,
*" width="220" height="220"
    backgroundColor="blue">
    <Label text="Row: 0; Column 0" row="0" col="0"
backgroundColor="yellow"></Label>
    <Label text="Row: 0; Column 1" row="0" col="1"
colSpan="1" backgroundColor="brown"></Label>
    <Label text="Row: 1; Column 0" row="1" col="0"
rowSpan="1" backgroundColor="red"></Label>
```

```
    <Label text="Row: 1; Column 1" row="1" col="1"
backgroundColor="red"></Label>
</GridLayout>
```

StackLayout

StackLayout arranges its children in a one-dimensional line that can be horizontally or vertically oriented. It may be sized using layout choices based on the available space in the layout. It features an orientation property that may determine whether the direction should be horizontal or vertical.

Let us add a StackLayout container to our application's home page as seen below:

```
<ActionBar>
    <Label text="Home"></Label>
</ActionBar>
<StackLayout orientation="vertical" width="210"
height="210" backgroundColor="blue">
    <Label text="Label1" width="40" height="40"
backgroundColor="green"></Label>
    <Label text="Label2" width="40" height="40"
backgroundColor="brown"></Label>
    <Label text="Label3" width="40" height="40"
backgroundColor="red"></Label>
    <Label text="Label4" width="40" height="40"
backgroundColor="orange"></Label>
</StackLayout>
```

WrapLayout

WrapLayout is a layout that is used to wrap information on new rows or columns.

It possesses the three qualities listed below:

- **orientation:** Display the information horizontally or vertically.

- **itemWidth:** itemWidth specifies the layout width for each child.

- **itemHeight:** itemHeight specifies the layout height for each child.

Let us add the WrapLayout container to our application's main page as seen below:

```
<ActionBar>
    <Label text="Home"></Label>
```

```
</ActionBar> <WrapLayout orientation="horizontal"
width="200" height="200" backgroundColor="blue">
   <Label text="Label1" width="70" height="70"
backgroundColor="green"></Label>
   <Label text="Label2" width="70" height="70"
backgroundColor="brown"></Label
   <Label text="Label3" width="70" height="70"
backgroundColor="red"></Label>
   <Label text="Label4" width="70" height="70"
backgroundColor="orange"></Label>
</WrapLayout>
```

FlexboxLayout

One of the sophisticated layout container components is the FlexboxLayout container component. It allows us to produce simple layouts up to highly complicated and refined layouts. It is built with CSS Flexbox.

The FlexboxLayout component has several attributes, which are as follows:

1. **flexDirection:** It denotes the order in which the child components are placed. The following are the potential values for flexDirection:

   - **row:** child components are stacked one on top of the other.

   - **row-reverse:** row-reverse arranges child components side by side but in the other direction.

   - **column:** child components are stacked one on top of the other.

   - **column-reverse:** child components are organized in a column-reverse fashion, one below the other but in the opposite direction.

   Let us add the FlexLayout container to our application's homepage as seen below:

```
<ActionBar>
   <Label text="Home"></Label>
</ActionBar>
<FlexboxLayout flexDirection="row">
   <Label text="First Item"
backgroundColor="yellow"></Label>
   <Label text="Second Item"
backgroundColor="red"></Label>
```

```
    <Label text="Third Item"
backgroundColor="green"></Label>
    <Label text="Fourth Item"
backgroundColor="red"></Label>
    <Label text="Fifth Item"
backgroundColor="yellow"></Label>
</FlexboxLayout>
```

Change the flexDirection value from row to row-reverse and see how it impacts the layout.

```
<ActionBar>
    <Label text="Home"></Label>
</ActionBar> <FlexboxLayout
flexDirection="row-reverse">
    <Label text="First Item"
backgroundColor="yellow"></Label>
    <Label text="Second Item"
backgroundColor="red"></Label>
    <Label text="Third Item"
backgroundColor="green"></Label>
    <Label text="Fourth Item"
backgroundColor="yellow"></Label>
    <Label text="Fifth Item"
backgroundColor="orange"></Label>
</FlexboxLayout>
```

Let's try changing the flexDirection value from row-reverse to column to see how it impacts the layout:

```
<ActionBar>
    <Label text="Home"></Label>
</ActionBar>
<FlexboxLayout flexDirection="column">
    <Label text="First Item"
backgroundColor="green"></Label>
    <Label text="Second Item"
backgroundColor="red"></Label>
    <Label text="Third Item"
backgroundColor="yellow"></Label>
    <Label text="Fourth Item"
backgroundColor="red"></Label>
    <Label text="Fifth Item"
backgroundColor="green"></Label>
</FlexboxLayout>
```

Let's try changing the flexDirection value from column to column-reverse and see how it impacts the layout:

```
<ActionBar>
    <Label text="Home"></Label>
</ActionBar>
<FlexboxLayout flexDirection="column-reverse">
    <Label text="First Item"
backgroundColor="green"></Label>
    <Label text="Second Item"
backgroundColor="red"></Label>
    <Label text="Third Item"
backgroundColor="yellow"></Label>
    <Label text="Fourth Item"
backgroundColor="red"></Label>
    <Label text="Fifth Item"
backgroundColor="green"></Label>
</FlexboxLayout>
```

2. **flexWrap:** It specifies whether the child components will be shown in a single row/column or will flow into several rows by wrapping in the direction specified by flexDirection.

   The following are the potential values:

   - **wrap:** If no space is available in the specified direction, wrap the child components (flexDirection).

   - **wrap-reverse:** The same as a wrap, except the component flow is in the other direction.

   Add the flexWrap property and set its value to wrap. Also, as seen below, add three more children:

```
<ActionBar>
    <Label text="Home"></Label>
&tl;/ActionBar>
<FlexboxLayout flexDirection="row"
flexWrap="wrap">
    <Label text="First Item"
backgroundColor="green"></Label>
    <Label text="Second Item"
backgroundColor="red"></Label>
    <Label text="Third Item"
backgroundColor="yellow"></Label>
```

```
    <Label text="Fourth Item"
backgroundColor="red"></Label>
    <Label text="Fifth Item"
backgroundColor="green"></Label>
    <Label text="Sixth Item"
backgroundColor="red"></Label>
    <Label text="Seventh Item"
backgroundColor="green"></Label>
    <Label text="Eighth Item"
backgroundColor="red"></Label>
</FlexboxLayout>
```

3. **JustifyContent:** It depicts how child components are placed in relation to one another and the overall structure. It has three properties, which are listed below:

   - **flex-end:** It pushes the child component to the end of the line.

   - **space-between:** It packs the child component by distributing it evenly in line.

   - **space-around:** Similar to space-between, except it packs the child component by evenly distributing it in line and equal space surrounding it.

   Let us also include justifyContent and see how it behaves:

```
<ActionBar>
    <Label text="Home"></Label>
</ActionBar>
<FlexboxLayout flexDirection="row" flexWrap="wrap"
justifyContent="space-around">
    <Label text="First Item"
backgroundColor="green"></Label>
    <Label text="Second Item"
backgroundColor="red"></Label>
    <Label text="Third Item"
backgroundColor="green"></Label>
    <Label text="Fourth Item"
backgroundColor="yellow"></Label>
    <Label text="Fifth Item"
backgroundColor="green"></Label>
    <Label text="Sixth Item"
backgroundColor="red"></Label>
```

```
    <Label text="Seventh Item"
backgroundColor="yellow"></Label>
    <Label text="Eighth Item"
backgroundColor="red"></Label>
</FlexboxLayout>
```

The FlexLayout container adds two new parameters for its children to control the order and shrinkability. These are their names:

- **order:** It sets the order in which the FlexLayout container's children will be displayed.

- **flexShrink:** It determines the children's ability to shrink to level 0.

In this chapter, we learned about NativeScript's introduction, how NativeScript apps are made, why NativeScript is significant, and what sorts of apps may be created with NativeScript. We also discussed NativeScript's benefits, features, and operation. We also spoke about installation and architecture. In addition, we learned about Angular application in NativeScript.

CHAPTER 2

Structuring Your App

IN THIS CHAPTER

> Pages and navigation

> Understanding the basics of app layouts

> Using advanced layouts

> Styling NativeScript apps

In the last chapter, we learned about NativeScript's architecture, installation, and use. This chapter will teach us about pages, navigation, layout, and how to style apps in NativeScript.

NAVIGATION IN NativeScript

Users may utilize the navigation to swiftly swipe in to their preferred screen, move across an app, or complete a specific activity. The navigation component assists us in implementing navigation from simple button clicks to more complicated patterns.

The navigation differs significantly between the core and angular versions of NativeScript. While the core framework navigation is the foundation for the navigation process, NativeScript's Angular model incorporates and extends the core navigation notion to make it compatible with the Angular framework.

In this section, we'll look at both basic navigation concepts and angular navigation adoption.

DOI: 10.1201/9781003299394-2

Fundamental Ideas

In this section, we'll look at how navigation works in core NativeScript.

NativeScript divides navigation into four categories depending on the direction it applies:

- Forward navigation
- Backward navigation
- Lateral navigation
- Bottom navigation

Forward Navigation

Forward navigation refers to directing users to the next level of hierarchy. It's built using two NativeScript components: Frame and Page.

Frame The root level component for navigation is the frame. It is not a visible container, but it serves as a container for page transitions.

As an example, consider the following:

```
<Frame id="featured" defaultPage="featured-page" />
```

Here,

Frame navigates to and renders the featured-page page component.

Page The Page component is located next to the Frame component and serves as a container for the user interface (UI) component. A simple example is shown below:

```
<Page loaded="onPageLoaded">
    <ActionBar title="Item" class="action-bar"></
ActionBar>
    <AbsoluteLayout>
        <Label text="label"/<
        <Button text="navigate('another-page')"
tap="onTap"/>
    </AbsoluteLayout>
</Page>
```

Here, initially, Page loads and produces all of the UI components of the screen.

When the user hits the button, they will be sent to another page.

Backward Navigation

The reverse navigation mechanism allows for backward travel via screens within the same app or across apps. It is the total opposite of forward navigation. To return to the previous page, use the simple goBack() function.

It is defined as follows:

```
<Page class="page" loaded="onPageLoaded">
    <ActionBar title="Item" class="action-bar">
</ActionBar>
    <StackLayout class="home-panel">
        <Button class="btn btn-primary" text="Hack"
tap="doHack"/>
    </StackLayout>
</Page>
```

Here,

When the user touches the button, the goBack() function is called. If a previous page is accessible, goBack() returns the user to it.

Lateral Navigation

Lateral navigation is the movement of displays at the same level of hierarchy. It is built on the hub pattern. BottomNavigation, Tabs, TabView, SideDrawer, and Modal View are the navigation components that enable it.

A basic example is as follows:

```
<Page class="pages" xmlns="http://www.nativescript.
org/tns.xsd">
    <ActionBar title="Hub" class="action-bar">
</ActionBar>
    <StackLayout class="home-panel">
        <Button class="btn btn-primary"
text="navigate('featuredpage')"
tap="navigateToFeatured" />
        <Button class="btn btn-primary"
text="navigate('searchpage')" tap="navigateToSearch" />
    </StackLayout>
</Page>
```

The navigateToFeatured function here uses the navigate() method to direct the visitor to the featured page.

Similarly, the navigateToSearch function takes the user to the search page.

The hub page may also be visited using the navigate method on the page screen, and the goBack() function can be used to exit the hub page.

As an example, consider the following:

```
<Page class="page">
  <ActionBar title="Item" class="action-bar">
</ActionBar>
  <StackLayout class="home-panel">
      <Button class="btn btn-primary"
text="navigate('hubpage')" tap="navigateToHub" />
      <Button class="btn btn-primary" text="doHack()"
tap="doHack" />
  </StackLayout>
</Page>
```

Bottom and Tab Navigation

Tab-based navigation is the most frequent type of navigation in mobile apps. The Tab navigation is either at the bottom of the screen or the top of the screen, below the header. It is accomplished by combining the TabView and BottomNavigation components.

Angular-Based Navigation

NativeScript's navigation paradigm is extended to suit the Angular routing idea. NativeScriptRouterModule is a new module created by extending Angular RouterModule.

The NativeScript angular navigation notion may be divided into the sections listed below:

- Page-router-outlet tag

- nsRouterLink attractive

- RouterExtension class

- Custom RouterReuseStrategy

In this part, we'll go through all of the angular navigation topics mentioned above.

Page-Router-Outlet
As previously stated, the page-router-outlet is Angular's replacement for the router-outlet. The page-router-outlet covers the NativeScript core navigation framework's Frame and Page strategy. Each page-router-outlet generates a new Frame component, and the outlet's defined components are wrapped in a Page component. The native navigate function is then used to travel to a different page or route.

Router Link (nsRouterLink)
nsRouterLink is Angular's RouterLink substitute. It allows a UI component to use a route to link to another page. nsRouterLink additionally offers the following two options:

- **page Transition:** This property is used to control the animation of page transitions. True enables the default transition. False disables the transition. The transition is determined by specific variables such as slide, fadein, and so on.

- **clearHistory:** Boolean true clears nsRouterLink's navigation history.

Here's a basic example of code:

```
<Button text="Go Home" [nsRouterLink]="['/home']"
  pageTransition="slide" clearHistory="true">
</Button>
```

Router Extension
NativeScript provides the RouterExtensions class, which exposes the basic NativeScript navigation mechanism.

RouterExtensions exposes the following methods:

- back
- canGoBack
- navigateByUrl
- backToPreviousPage
- navigate
- canGoBackToPreviousPage

The following is a simple example of code utilizing RouterExtensions:

```
import { RouterExtensions } from "nativescript-
angular/router";
@Component({
   // .....
})
export class HomeComponent {
   constructor(private routerExtensions:
RouterExtensions) { }
}
```

Custom Route Reuse Strategy

To support the architecture of a mobile application, NativeScript employs a bespoke route reuse approach (RouterReuseStrategy). A mobile application varies from a web application in several ways.

For example, in a web application, the page can be deleted when the user navigates away from the page and recreates when the user navigates back to the page. However, with a mobile application, the page is saved and reused. These ideas are taken into account when constructing the routing concept.

Routes

A basic routing module in a NativeScript Angular application will look like this:

```
import { NgModule } from "@angular/core";
import { Routes } from "@angular/router";
import { NativeScriptRouterModule } from
"nativescript-angular/router";
import { HomeComponent } from "./home.component";
import { SearchComponent } from "./search.component";
const routes: Routes = [
   { path: "", redirectTo: "/home", pathMatch: "full"
},
   { path: "home", component: HomeComponent },
   { path: "search", component: SearchComponent },
];
@NgModule({
   imports: [NativeScriptRouterModule.
forRoot(routes)],
```

```
    exports: [NativeScriptRouterModule]
})
export class AppRoutingModule { }
```

Here,

Except for a few differences, the routing module is relatively identical to the Angular version. In actuality, NativeScript exposes its primary navigation technique in a manner comparable to the Angular framework.

EVENTS HANDLING IN NativeScript

Events play a critical role in facilitating user interaction in any GUI program. When a user interacts with the application, an event is triggered, and a matching action is performed.

For example, the login procedure is initiated when a user hits the Login button on an application's login page.

Two people are involved in events:

- **Event sender:** The real event is raised by the event sender object.

- **Event listener:** Event listener is a function that listens for a particular event and executes it when it occurs.

Observable Class

It is a predefined class for dealing with events. It is defined further down:

```
const Observable = require("tns-core-modules/data/
observable").Observable;
```

Almost every object in NativeScript inherits from the Observable class, and hence every object supports events.

Event Listener

This section will learn how to build an object and add an event listener to it.

- **Step 1:** Create a button that is used to produce an event in the manner shown below:

  ```
  const Button = require("tns-core-modules/ui/
  button").Button;
  const testButton = new Button();
  ```

- **Step 2:** Then, as seen below, add text to the button:

```
testButton.text = "Click";
```

- **Step 3:** Create a function called onTap as shown below:

```
let onTap = function(args) {
    console.log("clicked!");
};
```

- **Step 4:** Attach the tap event to the onTap function as seen below:

```
testButton.on("tap", onTap, this);
```

An alternative method for adding an event listener is as follows:

```
testButton.addEventListener("tap", onTap, this);
```

- **Step 5:** An alternate method of attaching an event is through the UI itself, as detailed below:

```
<Button text="click" (tap)="onTap($event)"></Button>
```

Here,

$event is of the EventData type in this case. EventData has two properties, which are as follows:

1. **Object:** An observable instance used to trigger an event. It is the Button object in this situation.

2. **EventName:** This is the name of the event. It is a tap event in this circumstance.

- **Step 6:** Finally, as mentioned below, an event listener can be detached/removed at any moment:

```
testButton.off(Button.onTap);
```

We can also use the following format:

```
testButton.removeEventListener(Button.onTap);
```

Modifying BlankNgApp

Let's change the BlankNgApp app to grasp the NativeScript events better.

- **Step 1:** Open the UI for the home component, src/app/home/home. component.html, and add the following code:

```
<ActionBar>
    <Label text="Home"></Label>
</ActionBar>
```

```
<StackLayout>
   <Button text='Fire event' class="-primary"
color='white' (tap)='onButtonTap($event)'>
</Button>
</StackLayout>
```

Here,

The event is represented by tap, while Button represents the event raiser.

The event listener is onButtonTap.

- **Step 2:** Open the code for the home component, "src/app/home/ home.component.ts," and edit the code below:

```
import { Component, OnInit } from "@angular/
core";
import { EventData } from "tns-core-modules/data/
observable";
import { Button } from "tns-core-modules/ui/
button"
@Component({
   selector: "Home",
   templateUrl: "./home.component.html"
})
export class HomeComponent implements OnInit {
   constructor() {
      // Use the component constructor to inject
providers.
   }
   ngOnInit(): void {
      // Init your component properties here.
   }
   onButtonTap(args: EventData): void {
      console.log(args.eventName);
      const button = <Button>args.object;
      console.log(button.text);
   }
}
```

Here,

A new event listener, onButtonTap, has been added.

In the console, print the event name, tap and button text, and fire an event.

- **Step 3:** Start the app and press the button. It outputs the following line to the console:

```
LOG from device <device name>: tap
LOG from device <device name>: Fire an event
```

DATA BINDING IN NativeScript

One of the advanced ideas provided by NativeScript is data binding. NativeScript adheres as closely as possible to the Angular data binding idea. Data binding allows the UI component to display/update the current value of the application data model without the need for scripting.

NativeScript allows for two types of data binding. They are listed below:

- **One-way data binding:** When the model changes, the UI is updated.

- **Two-way data binding:** Sync the UI and the model. When the model is changed, the UI is immediately updated, and when the UI receives data from the user (the UI is updated), the model is likewise updated.

In this part, we'll go through both notions.

One-Way Data Binding

To allow one-way data binding in a UI component, NativeScript provides a simple option. To enable one-way data binding, just include a square bracket in the target UI's property and then assign it the relevant model's property.

To edit the text content of a Label component, for example, just change the UI code as follows:

```
<Label [text]='this.model.prop' />
```

Here,

The term "this.model.prop" refers to the model's property, this.model.

Let's modify our BlankNgApp to understand one-way data binding better.

- **Step 1:** Create a new model, User (src/model/user.ts), as shown below:

```
export class User {
    name: string
}
```

- **Step 2:** Open the UI for our component, src/app/home/home.com-ponent.html, and make the following changes to the code:

```
<ActionBar>
   <Label text="Home"></Label>
</ActionBar>
<GridLayout columns="*" rows="auto, auto, auto">
   <Button text="Click-here to greet" class="-
primary" color='gray'
      (tap)='onButtonTap($event)' row='1'
column='0'>
   </Button>
   <Label [text]='this.user.name' row='2'
column='0'
      height="40px" textAlignment='center'
style='font-size: 15px;
      font-weight: bold; margin: 0px 32px 0
25px;'>
   </Label>
</GridLayout>
```

Here,

The text of the Label is set to the property name of the user model in this case.

The onButtonTap method is associated with the button tap event.

- **Step 3:** Open the code for the home component, src/app/home/home. component.ts, and make the changes shown below:

```
import { Component, OnInit } from "@angular/core";
import { User } from "../../model/user"
@Component({
   selector: "Home",
   templateUrl: "./home.component.html"
})
export class HomeComponent implements OnInit {
   public user: User;
   constructor() {
      // Use the component constructor to inject
providers.
      this.user = new User();
      this.user.name = "User1";
   }
   ngOnInit(): void {
```

```
        // Init your component properties here.
    }
    onButtonTap(args: EventData) {
        this.user.name = 'User2';
    }
}
```

Here,

The user model is imported.

The constructor of the component creates the user object.

The onButtonTap event has been implemented. onButtonTap implementation The User object is updated, and the property's name is changed to User2.

- **Step 4:** Compile and run the program, then click the button to change the model, and the Label text will be changed automatically. The application's initial and final states will also change.

Two-Way Data Binding

For sophisticated functionality, NativeScript also supports two-way data binding. It ties the model data to the UI and the data changed in the UI to the model.

To do two-way data binding, utilize the ngModel property and surround it with [] and (), as seen below:

```
<TextField [(ngModel)] = 'this.user.name'></TextField>
```

To further understand the two-way data binding, let's modify the BlankNgApp application.

- **Step 1:** Import the NativeScriptFormsModule into the HomeModule (src/app/home/home.module.ts) as shown below:

```
import { NgModule, NO_ERRORS_SCHEMA } from
"@angular/core";
import { NativeScriptCommonModule } from
"nativescript-angular/common";
import { HomeRoutingModule } from "./home-routing.
module";
import { HomeComponent } from "./home.component";
import { NativeScriptFormsModule } from
"nativescript-angular/forms";
```

```
@NgModule({
    imports: [
        NativeScriptCommonModule,
        HomeRoutingModule,
        NativeScriptFormsModule
    ],
    declarations: [
        HomeComponent
    ],
    schemas: [
        NO_ERRORS_SCHEMA
    ]
})
export class HomeModule { }
```

The NativeScriptFormsModule supports two-way data binding in this case. Otherwise, the two-way data binding will not function properly.

- **Step 2:** Modify the UI of the home component as shown below:

```
<ActionBar> <Label text="Home"></Label>
</ActionBar>
<GridLayout columns="*" rows="auto, auto">
    <TextField hint="Username" row='0' column='0'
color="white"
        backgroundColor="lightyellow" height="74px"
[(ngModel)]='this.user.name'>
    </TextField>
    <Label [text]='this.user.name' row='1'
column='0' height="40px"
        textAlignment='center' style='font-size:
14px; font-weight: bold;
        margin: 0px 32px 0 25px;'>
    </Label>
</GridLayout>
```

Here,

The text attribute of the Label component is set to one-way data binding. If the model user is modified, the text property will also be updated.

The ngModel is assigned to this.user.name by the TextField component. If the model user is modified, the text property will also be updated. Simultaneously, if the user changes TextField's value, the model is updated. When the model is modified, the text attribute of the Label is also changed. As a result, if the user modifies the data, it will be shown in the Label's text attribute.

- **Step 3:** Start the program and try changing the value of the text field. The application's initial and final states will be comparable.

MODULES FOR NativeScript

A NativeScript module is a collection of linked features packed into a single library. Let's have a look at the NativeScript framework's modules.

It includes the NativeScript framework's fundamental functionality. Let's go through the main modules in this session.

Application

The application includes platform-specific mobile application implementation. A basic core module is defined below:

```
const applicationModule = require("tns-core-modules/
application");
```

Console

Messages are logged using the Console module. It employs the following methods:

```
console.log("My FirstApp project");
console.info("Native apps!");
console.warn("Warning message!");
console.error("Exception occurred");
```

Application-settings

The application-settings module offers a way for managing application settings. To include this module, we must include the following code:

```
const appSettings = require("tns-core-modules/
application-settings");
```

The following are a few techniques accessible in the application-setting:

- **setBoolean (key: string, value: boolean):** creates a boolean object.

- **setNumber(key: string, value: number):** creates a number object.

- **setString(); (key: string, value: string):** creates a string object.

- **getAllKeys():** returns a list of all keys that have been saved.

- **hasKey(key: string):** determines whether or not a key is present.

- **Clean:** removes all previously saved values.

- **Delete:** deletes any entry depending on the key.

The following is a simple example of an application setting:

```
function onNavigatingTo(args) {
   appSettings.setBoolean("isTurnedOff", false);
   appSettings.setString("name", "nativescript");
   appSettings.setNumber("locationX", 54.321);
   const isTurnedOn = appSettings.
getBoolean("isTurnedOn");
   const username = appSettings.getString("username");
   const locationX = appSettings.
getNumber("locationX");
   // if there is no value for "noKey" return "not
present"
   const someKey = appSettings.getString("noKey",
"not-present");
}
exports.onNavigatingTo = onNavigatingTo;
function onClear() {
   // Removing single entry
   appSettings.remove("isTurnedOff");
   // Clearing whole settings
   appSettings.clear();
}
```

- **http:** This module handles http requests and responses. Add the following code to our application to include this module:

  ```
  const httpModule = require("tns-core-modules/http");
  ```

- **getString:** This method is used to perform a request and download data from a URL as a string. It is defined further down:

  ```
  httpModule.getString("https://.../get").then(
     (r) => {
        viewModel.set("getStringResult", r);
     }, (e) =>
  ```

```
        {
        }
    );
```

- **getJSON:** It is used to access JSON data. It is defined further down:

```
httpModule.getJSON("https://.../get").then((r) => {
}, (e) => {
});
```

- **getImage:** Downloads the specified URL's content and returns an ImageSource object. It is defined further down:

```
httpModule.getImage("https://.../image/jpeg")
.then((r) => {
}, (e) => {
});
```

- **getFile:** It takes two arguments: the URL and the file location.

  - **URL:** The data is downloaded.

- **File path:** Save URL data to a file using the file path. It is defined as follows:

```
httpModule.getFile("https://").then((resultFile)
=> {
}, (e) => {
});
```

- **request:** It has a choice argument. Its purpose is to request options and provide an HttpResponse object. It is defined as follows:

```
httpModule.request({
    url: "https://.../get",
    method: "GET"
}).then((response) => {
}, (e) => {
});
```

Image-source

The image-source module is used to store the picture. We may add this module using the following statement:

```
const imageSourceModule = require("tns-core-modules/
image-source");
```

If we wish to load pictures from a resource, use the code below:

```
const imgFromResources = imageSourceModule
.fromResource("icon");
```

Use the command below to add a picture from a local file:

```
const folder = fileSystemModule.knownFolders
.currentApp();
const path = fileSystemModule.path.join(folder.path,
"images/sample1.png");
const imageFromLocalFile = imageSourceModule
.fromFile(path);
```

Use the command below to save a picture to a file path:

```
const img = imageSourceModule.fromFile(imagePath);
const folderDest = fileSystemModule.knownFolders.
documents();
const pathDest = fileSystemModule.path.
join(folderDest.path, "sample1.png");
const saved = img.saveToFile(pathDest, "png"); if
(saved) {
    console.log(" sample image saved successfully!");
}
```

Timer

This module is used to run programs at specific time intervals. To do so, we'll need to utilize require:

```
const timerModule = require("tns-core-modules/
timer");
```

It is based on two approaches.

- **setTimeout:** This function is used to postpone the execution. It is measured in milliseconds.

- **setInterval:** This method is used to apply to repeat at predefined intervals.

Trace

This module can be used for debugging. It provides logging information. This module can be denoted as:

```
const traceModule = require("tns-core-modules/
trace");
```

If we wish to activate it in your application, use the command below:

```
traceModule.enable();
```

ui/image-cache

Image download requests are handled by the image-cache module, which caches downloaded images. This module is illustrated as follows:

```
const Cache = require("tns-core-modules/ui/image-
cache").Cache;
```

Connectivity

This module is used to receive the connected network's connection information. It can be written as:

```
const connectivityModule = require("tns-core-modules/
connectivity");
```

Modules of Functionality

A large number of system/platform specific modules are included in functionality modules. The following are some of the essential modules:

- **platform:** A platform is used to display information about our device. It can be defined as follows:

  ```
  const platformModule = require("tns-core-modules/
  platform");
  ```

- **fps-meter:** A tool that measures the number of frames per second. It can be defined as follows:

  ```
  const fpsMeter = require("tns-core-modules/
  fps-meter");
  ```

- **file-system:** This function is used to interact with our device's file system. It is defined further down:

```
const fileSystemModule = require("tns-core-modules/file-system");
```

- **ui/gestures:** This is used to work with UI gestures.

The Module of UI

The UI component and its associated capabilities are included in the UI module. The following are some of the essential UI modules:

- frame

- page

- animation

- text/formatted-string

- xml

- color

- styling

PLUGINS FOR NativeScript

The npm package is used to provide native functionality to a project. We may use this package to install, search for, and uninstall plugins. This section goes into great detail on plugins.

Commands:

- **add:** It's used to install plugins.

- **update:** This function updates the given plugin and modifies its dependencies.

- **remove:** Uninstall the plugin.

- **build:** This command is used to create plugins for iOS or Android projects.

- **create:** This command generates a plugin for your project.

Adding Plugins

The syntax shown below is used to create a new plugin:

```
tns plugin add <plugin-name>
```

For example, if we want to include nativescript-barcodescanner, we may use the code below:

```
tns plugin add nativescript-barcodescanner
```

We may also use npm module to add the plugin mentioned above:

```
npm install nativescript-barcodescanner
```

NativeScript CLI now fetches the plugin from npm and installs it in our node modules folder.

If we want to directly add the plugin to our package.json and avoid any dependency concerns, use the following command instead of the previous one:

```
npm i nativescript-barcodescanner
```

If we wish to install developer requirements while developing, use the code below:

```
npm i tns-platform-declarations --save-dev
```

Here,

tns-platform-declarations is a developer dependency that is only necessary for intelliSense during development.

Importing Plugins

We have now installed the nativescript-barcodescanner plugin. Let us insert the following command into our project:

```
const maps = require("nativescript-barcodescanner");
maps.requestPermissions();
```

Updating Plugins

This approach updates a specific plugin by uninstalling the previous version, installing the new version, and modifying its dependencies. It is defined further down:

```
tns plugin update <Plugin name version>
```

Removing Plugin

If we wish to uninstall the plugin, use the syntax below if it is not necessary:

```
tns plugin remove <plugin-name>
```

For example, if we wish to remove the previously installed nativescript-google-maps-sdk, use the command below:

```
tns plugin remove nativescript-barcodescanner
```

We could see the following response:

```
Successfully removed plugin
nativescript-barcodescanner
```

Building Plugins

It generates the plugin's Android-specific project files, which may be found at platforms/android. Let us create the nativescript-barcodescanner plugin using the command below:

```
tns plugin build nativescript-barcodescanner
```

Creating Plugins

NativeScript plugins are specific JavaScript modules. It is defined in the srcpackage.json file of our application. This module is used to build a new project for the creation of NativeScript plugins. It is defined further down:

```
tns plugin create <Plugin Repository Name> [--path
<Directory>]
```

NATIVE APIs USING JavaScript

This section provides an overview of how to use JavaScript to access Native APIs.

Marshaling

For both Android and iOS platforms, the NativeScript Runtime supports implicit type conversion. This is referred to as marshaling. NativeScript-iOS platform, for example, may implicitly translate JavaScript and Objective-C data types, and Java/Kotlin can be readily mapped to JavaScript project types and values. Let's take a quick look at how to marshal in each category.

Numeric Values

We can simply convert numeric data types from iOS and Android to JavaScript numbers. The following defines a simple number translation for iOS into JavaScript:

```
console.log('max(6,9) = ${max(6,9)}');
```

Here,

The JavaScript number is converted from the native max() method.

Android Environment

Java offers a variety of numeric types, including byte, short, int, float, double, and long. JavaScript only supports the numeric type.

Consider the following simple Java class:

```
class Demo extends java.lang.Object {
    public int maxMethod(int c,int d) {
        if(c>d) {
            return c;
        } else {
            return d;
        }
    }
}
```

The preceding code has two integer parameters. We may use JavaScript to invoke the above code object, as demonstrated below:

```
//Create an instance for the Demo class
var obj = new Demo();

//implicit integer conversion for calling the above
method
obj.maxMethod(6,9);
```

Strings

Strings for Android are defined in java.lang.string, while strings for iOS are specified in NSSring. Let's take a look at how to marshal on both platforms.

Android

Strings are immutable; however, String buffers can handle mutable strings.
   An example of basic mapping is shown in the code below:

```
//Create widget of android label
var label = new android.widget.Label();

// JavaScript string Create
var str = "Label1";

//Convertion of JavaScript string into java label
.setText(str);
// text converted to java.lang.String
```

Java.lang.Boolean defines the Boolean class. This class encapsulates a boolean value in an object. We can convert boolean to String and vice versa with ease. A simple example is shown below:

```
// java string creation
let data = new java.lang.String('NativeScript');

//map of java String to JavaScript string,
let result = data.startsWith('N');

// result return
console.log(result);// true
```

iOS Environment

Although the NSString class is immutable, its subclass NSMutableString is not. This class includes a set of methods for interacting with strings. It is said as follows:

```
class NSString : NSObject
```

Consider the following objective-c declaration:

```
NSString *str = @"nativescript";
```

```
// the string to uppercase convertion
NSString *str1;
str1 = [str uppercaseString];
NSLog(@"Uppercase String : %@\n", str1 );
```

JavaScript strings can be simply mapped to NSStrings.

Arrays

This section describes how to implement array marshaling. Let's start with an example from the iOS ecosystem.

Declaration of an Array

```
class NSArray : NSObject
```

In this case, NSArray is utilized to handle an ordered collection of objects known as arrays. It's used to make a static array. NSMutableArray, a sub-class of it, is used to build dynamic arrays.

Consider the following: NSArray objects may be built using array literals:

```
let array: NSArray = ["React","Vue","TypeScript"]
```

Now, as seen below, we can map this array into JavaScript.

```
// native array creation
let nsArr = NSArray.arrayWithArray("React","Vue","Type
Script"]);

// simple javascript array creation
let jsArr = ["Hello,World","NativeScript"];

//compare the two arrays,
let compare = nsArr.isEqual(jsArr);
console.log(comapre);
```

Array Declaration in Android

Arrays in Java are defined in java.util.Arrays. This class offers different array manipulation methods. An example is shown below:

```
//javascript array
let data = [13,46,22,54,32,79,51];
```

```
// java array creation
let result = ns.example.Math.maxElement(data);
console.log(result);
```

Classes and Objects

Object-Oriented Programming's fundamental ideas are classes and objects. Class is a prototype that the user has defined. An object is a class instance. A class is a collection of attributes or methods common to all objects of the same kind. Let's look at native classes and objects in both mobile development environments.

Android Environment

The whole package name serves as a unique identification for Java and Kotlin classes.

As an example:

android.view.View: It is a simple UI class for screen layout and user interaction. This class may be accessed using JavaScript, as illustrated below:

```
const View = android.view.View;
```

First, we import the class using the following expression:

```
import android.view.View;
```

Then, as seen below, build a class:

```
public class MyClass {
    public static void staticMethod(context) {
        // view instance creation
        android.view.View myview = new android.view.
View(context);
    }
}
```

We may access JavaScript functions in the class mentioned above by using the code below:

```
const myview = new android.view.View(context);
```

Similarly, within java.lang packages, we may access interfaces, constants, and enumerations.

iOS Environment

Classes in Objective-C are divided into two sections: @interface and @implementation. The term @interface is followed by the name of the interface(class) in the class specification. All classes in Objective-C are derived from the fundamental class NSObject.

It is the superclass class for all Objective-C classes. The Simple Circle class is defined as follows:

```
@interface Circle:NSObject {
    //Instance-variable
    int radius;
}
@end
```

Consider the following class, which has only one method:

```
@interface MyClass : NSObject
+ (void)baseStaticMethod;
@end
```

The code below may be used to convert this class to javascript:

```
function MyClass() { /* native call */ };
Object.setPrototypeOf(MyClass, NSObject);
BaseClass.baseStaticMethod = function () { /* native
call */ };
```

The instanceof operator in JavaScript is used to determine whether an object derives from a specific class. This can be expressed as:

```
var obj = MyClass.alloc().init(); // creation of
object
console.log(obj instanceof NSObject); //return
value(true)
```

In this case, Objective-C objects are created with the alloc, init, or new methods. In the above example, we can easily generate object initialization by utilizing the new method as shown below:

```
var obj = MyClass.new();
```

Static methods and properties can also be accessed in the same way.

NativeScript – ANDROID APPLICATION DEVELOPMENT

When we create and publish our app, it becomes available to all users. Google Play is a well-developed publishing platform. It allows us to publish and distribute our Android applications to individuals around the globe. This session will walk through the process of publishing our Native app to Google Play.

Sidekick for NativeScript

SideKick is a graphical UI client that works with all operating systems. It streamlines the NativeScript CLI process and aids in the development of mobile applications.

Publish Our Sidekick App to Google Play Console

The download and installation of sidekick are dependent on our operating system. To run our app in Sidekick, follow the steps below:

- **Step 1: Launch Sidekick**

- **Step 2: Create our device**

  Now, run our app on your smartphone and pick the build option from the toolbar, then Android.

- **Step 3: Properties**

  Select the properties tab and add our Android setup.

- **Step 4: Plugins**

  Sidekick assists us in determining which plugins rely on for our application. Select the Plugins tab.

- **Step 5: Android certificates**

  Click the cogwheel icon on Android and select Browse, then choose a certificate from our file system.

  Close the dialogue box when we've made our selection.

- **Step 6: Build our application**

  Finally, from the build, choose local build, and then from the configuration drop-down menu, select release. After that, we'll create our application.

- **Step 7: Application package**

  When the build is finished, it will produce a directory and an apk file. Save the application package's location. This apk file is needed to upload to Google Play.

- **Step 8: Publish in Google Play**

  Select Google Play from the toolbar's publish option. Then, in the Manage Android Certificates for Google Play Store window, click Add.

  Then, choose Build type and enter our Service Account JSON key, select Alpha, Beta, or Production tracks, and click Upload.

Publish Our App to Google Play

To publish our app on Google Play Console, we must first complete the following requirements:

- We must be logged in to Google Play.

- We have a Google Play self-signed code signing identity that is valid.

Procedure for Releasing our App

The methods below will help us understand how to publish our app on the Google Play store.

- **Step 1: Access the Google Play console**

  Open the Google Play interface and sign in with our Google account.

- **Step 2: Develop an app**

  Create a new app by going to the All Applications page and clicking Create Application. Now, add the default language, application title, and finally click go to begin.

- **Step 3: Complete the essential fields**

  Navigate to the shop listing page, fill in the appropriate data, and finish the required assets and save all changes.

- **Step 4: Determine a price and a distribution strategy**

  Go to the Pricing and Distribution page, complete all of the parameters, and save all our changes.

- **Step 5: Release your app**

  Select Alpha, Beta from the App Releases tab. It is used to put our application through its paces. Also, choose Production tracks. It's utilized to get our software onto Google Play. Finally, include the application package (apk).

- **Step 6: Review our app**

  This is the last step. Check the Review to see if there are any problems. If there are no difficulties, confirm rollout to publish our app.

OUR FIRST APPLICATION

Make our First NativeScript Application:

From setting up our development environment to launching the app on our device, We'll guide through the whole process of creating an app with NativeScript. Here's a synopsis of what I'll be talking about:

1. Installing NativeScript

2. Creating the app

3. Launching the app

4. Application debugging

We'll be operating the app, particularly on the Android platform. However, if we want to deploy to iOS, we can still follow along because the code will be identical. The only differences are in the process of installing NativeScript and the instructions that are executed when the program is launched.

Setting Up NativeScript

To get NativeScript up and running, we must first install Node.js. After installing Node.js, run npm install -g nativescript in your terminal to install the NativeScript command-line utility.

The last step is to install the development tool for each platform to which we intend to deploy. The Android SDK is what we're looking for if we're looking for a way to get started with Android. It's XCode for iOS. After configuring our environment, run tns doctor to ensure that it's ready for NativeScript development.

Note:

- Only Mac OS X computers may be used to build for iOS.

- To work with iOS devices and projects, we must have Mac OS X Mavericks or later.

- Our components are updated.

- There were no problems discovered.

There's a statement stating that we can only create for iOS on Mac OS X PCs. This implies that if we're using a PC, we can only deploy to Android devices. However, if we're working on a Mac, we'll be able to deploy to both the iOS and Android platforms.

If we run into any issues during the setup, we may request an invitation to the NativeScript Slack Community, and once there, head to the getting started to channel and express our concerns there.

Creating the APP

The app that we will create is a note-taking app. It will allow the user to make notes, each with the option of attaching a picture obtained with the device's camera. The notes are saved using NativeScript application settings and can be erased separately.

To begin, use the following command to generate a new NativeScript project:

```
tns create noter --appid "com.yourname.noter"
```

The project's name is noter, and the app ID is com.yourname.noter. This will be used to identify our software once submitted to the Play or App Store. The tns create command will automatically generate the following folders and files for us:

- app
- node_modules
- platforms
- package.json

Typically, we'll just need to touch the files in the app directory. Nevertheless, there may be situations when we need to make changes to files under the platforms/android directory. One example is when a plugin we're attempting to utilize does not immediately link the dependencies and files required.

Then, in the app directory, remove all files except the App Resources folder. After that, make the following files:

- app.js
- app.css
- notes-page.js
- notes-page.xml

These are the files that the NativeScript runtime will make use of .css files are used for style, and.js files are utilized for functionality, much like when constructing web pages. However, for the app's markup, we utilize XML rather than HTML. Typically, each app screen (e.g., login, sign up, or dashboard) would have its folder with XML, CSS, and JavaScript files. However, because our app has one screen, we generated all of the files in the root directory.

The Entry Point File

Open and Add the following code to the app.js file:

```
var application = require("application");
application.start({ moduleName: "notes-page" });
```

This is where a NativeScript application begins. It specifies the module used for the app's initial page using the application module and its start function. In this situation, we specified notes-page, which implies the module is notes-page.js, the markup is notes-page.xml, and the page style is notes-page.css. This is a NativeScript convention that requires all files for a single page to have same name.

UI Markup Adding

Open the notes-page.xml file and add the following code:

```
<Page xmlns="http://schemas.nativescript.org/tns.xsd"
loaded="pageLoaded">
    <Page.actionBar>
        <ActionBar title="{{ app_title }}">
            <ActionBar.actionItems>
                <ActionItem tap="newNote" ios.
position="left" android.position="actionBar">
                    <ActionItem.actionView>
                        <StackLayout
orientation="horizontal">
                            <Label text="New Item"
color="yellow" cssClass="header-item" />
                        </StackLayout>
                    </ActionItem.actionView>
                </ActionItem>
            </ActionBar.actionItems>
        </ActionBar>
    </Page.actionBar>
```

```
<StackLayout>
    <StackLayout id="form"
cssClass="form-container">
        <TextView text="{{ item_title }}"
hint="Title" />
        <Button text="Attach Image" cssClass="link
label" tap="openCamera" />
        <Image src="{{ img }}" id="img"
cssClass="image" visibility="{{ attachment_img?
'visible' : 'collapsed' }}" />
        <Button text="Note Save" tap="Notesave"
cssClass="primary-button" />
    </StackLayout>

    <ListView items="{{ notes }}" id="list"
visibility="{{ showForm?  'collapsed' : 'visible' }}">
        <ListView.itemTemplate>
            <GridLayout columns="*,*"
rows="auto,auto" cssClass="item">
                <Label text="{{ title's }}"
textWrap="true" row="0" col="0" />
                <Image src="{{ photo's }}"
horizontalAlignment="center"
verticalAlignment="center" cssClass="image" row="1"
col="0" visibility="{{ photo?  'visible' : 'collapsed'
}}" />
                <Button text="Delete" index="{{
index }}" cssClass="delete-button" tap="deleteNote"
row="0" col="1" horizontalAlignment="right"
loaded="btnLoaded" />
            </GridLayout>
        </ListView.itemTemplate>
    </ListView>
    </StackLayout>
</Page>
```

When building app pages in NativeScript, always begin with the <Page> tag. This is how NativeScript detects that we are attempting to create a new page. The xmlns property gives the URL to the XML file's schema.

If we go to the supplied schema URL, we will see the definitions of all the XML tags that we may use in NativeScript. The loaded property provides the function that will be run after the page has been loaded.

This function declaration will be examined later in the notes-page.js file.

```
<Page xmlns="http://schemas.nativescript.org/tns.xsd"
loaded="pageLoaded">
...
</Page>
```

By default, the app header merely contains the program's title. If we wanted to add other UI components, we'd have to redefine it using <Page.action-Bar>. Then, within, we describe what we wish to appear in the header. The title is given by using <ActionBar> and setting the title property to the desired page title.

The moustache syntax is used below to print the value of app title defined in the notes-page.js file. This is how we output values connected to a page.

```
<Page.actionBar>
    <ActionBar title="{{ app_title }}">
    ...

    </ActionBar>
</Page.actionBar>
```

To define buttons, use <ActionBar.actionItems> as the parent, and each ActionItem> will represent the buttons that we wish to specify. The tap property defines a method that will be run when the button is tapped, whereas os.position and android.position are the button's positions in iOS and Android, respectively.

We might utilize the text property of the <ActionItem> to provide the button text. However, at the moment, NativeScript does not support altering the text color of the button using CSS. As a result, we've used ActionItem.actionView> to specify the content of the button and set its text color instead.

```
<ActionBar.actionItems>
  <ActionItem tap="newNote" ios.position="left"
android.position="actionBar">
    <ActionItem.actionView>
        <StackLayout orientation="horizontal">
          <Label text="New Item" color="lightgrey"
cssClass="header-item" />
```

```
    </StackLayout>
  </ActionItem.actionView>
  </ActionItem>
</ActionBar.actionItems>
```

The actual page content comes afterward. We may organize the various elements by using one or more of the layout containers. We've utilized two of the possible layouts in the examples below StackLayout and GridLayout.

StackLayout allows us to stack all of the components included inside it. This layout's orientation is vertical by default; thus, each UI component is stacked below the last. Consider lego blocks in a downhill flow.

GridLayout, on the other hand, allows you to arrange components in a table structure. If we've used Bootstrap or other CSS grid frameworks before, this should seem intuitive. The GridLayout enables us to specify the rows and columns in which each UI component will be positioned.

We'll look into how this is done eventually. For the time being, let's get to the coding.

Let's start by defining the form for adding a new note. You may specify elements like id and cssClass (similar to HTML's class property) just as in HTML. If we wish to alter an element from code, the id attribute is associated with it. In our scenario, we want to animate the shape later. cssClass specifies the CSS class that will be used to style the element.

A text area for inputting the note title, a button for adding an image, the selected picture, and a button for saving the note are all included within the form.

The image element is only displayed if the attachment img property is set to true. If an image was previously connected, this will be the case.

```
<StackLayout id="form" cssClass="form-container">
  <TextView text="{{ item_title }}" hint="Title" />
  <Button text="Attach-Image" cssClass="link label"
tap="openCamera" />
  <Image src="{{ attachmentimg }}" id="attachmentimg"
cssClass="image" visibility="{{ attachment_img?
'visible' : 'collapsed' }}" />
  <Button text="Note Save" tap="saveNote"
cssClass="primary-button" />
</StackLayout>
```

Following that is a collection of the user's previously added notes. The ListView component is used to construct lists. Items are accepted as a necessary attribute. The value might be a simple array or an observable array.

A normal JavaScript array will suffice if we do not need to conduct any type of modification (e.g., deleting or updating a field) on each item in the array. Otherwise, utilize an observable array, which allows us to make changes to the array and have them automatically reflected in the UI.

It's also worth noting that a ListView may have an itemTap property, which allows us to define the function that should be called when a ListView item is tapped. However, we haven't truly included it in this case because we don't need to take any action when an item is tapped.

```
<ListView items="{{ notes }}" id="list" visibility="{{
showForm?  'collapsed' : 'visible' }}">
  ...
</ListView>
```

<ListView.itemTemplate> may be used to specify the items in the ListView. We're going to use a<GridLayout> to make two rows and two columns. The columns property is used to indicate the number of columns in each row.

In this situation, *,* indicates two columns, each taking up an equal amount of space in the current row. So, if the entire row is 300 pixels big, each column will be 150 pixels wide. So, each * symbolizes one column, and a comma separates each one.

The rows property is similar, except it regulates how much space a single row takes up. It will only take up the space required by the children of each row if it is set to auto.

After establishing the GridLayout's columns and rows, we must specify which of its children belongs to which row and column. The first row includes the item's title (1st column) and the delete button (2nd column). The picture that was connected to the item is shown in the second row (1st column). The row and column attributes for each element are used to specify the row and columns.

Take note of the use of horizontalAlignment and verticalAlignment as well. Consider this the NativeScript counterpart of the HTML text-align property. We're aligning UI components instead of text. VerticalAlignment may be set to top, bottom, center, or stretch, whereas horizontalAlignment can be set to right, left, center, or stretch. Most of them are self-explanatory, except for stretch, which expands to take up the available horizontal or vertical space.

HorizontalAlignment and verticalAlignment are used in this scenario to center the image both horizontally and vertically within its column.

And on the delete button, horizontalAlignment is used to align it to the right-most area of the second column.

```
<ListView.itemTemplate>
  <GridLayout columns="*,*" rows="auto,auto"
cssClass="item">
    <Label text="{{ title's }}" textWrap="true"
row="0" col="0" />
    <Image src="{{ photo's }}"
horizontalAlignment="center"
verticalAlignment="center" cssClass="image" row="1"
col="0" visibility="{{ photo? 'visible' : 'collapsed'
}}" />

    <Button text="Delete" index="{{ index }}"
cssClass="delete-button" tap="deleteNote" row="0"
col="1" horizontalAlignment="left" loaded="btnLoaded" />
  </GridLayout>
</ListView.itemTemplate>
```

The ListView does not have an itemTap property. Instead, we'd want to add a delete action that would be done a delete button anytime within a list item is touched. Each item has an index attribute, which we pass as a custom attribute to the delete button. This is the unique key used to identify each object to refer to it when needed simply.

Take note of the loaded property as well. Buttons can have a loaded property, much like <Page>. You'll see how this is utilized later.

JavaScript Code
Now we'll have a look at the JavaScript that makes everything work. We'll write the notes-page.js file in this part.

Initialization
First, we import the modules data/observable and data/observable-array. These are NativeScript built-in modules that allow us to construct observable objects and arrays. Observables enable us to update the UI as these objects and arrays change automatically.

PageArray is used in our program to store the array of notes, and page-Data connects it to the page. pageData additionally acts as a basic container for any data that will be displayed in the UI.

```
var Observable = require("data/observable");
var ObservableArray = require("data/
observable-array");
var pageArray = new ObservableArray.ObservableArray();
var pageData = new Observable.Observable({
    notes: pageArray
});
```

Import all of the additional modules that we'll be utilizing on this page next:

- **camera:** for use with the device's camera.

- **view:** used to refer to certain items on the page. Consider it the document's equivalent. In NativeScript, use getElementById.

- **ui/enums:** global dictionary of constant values for anything UI-related.

- **ui/animation:** used to animate items.

- **application-settings:** used for storing local data.

- **file-system:** used to work with the filesystem.

```
var cameraModule = require("camera");
var view = require("ui/core/view");
var uiEnums = require("ui/enums");
var animation = require("ui/animation");
var appSettings = require("application-settings");
var fs = require("file-system");
```

Then, set the values for the variables that will be used throughout the file. page is used to store a reference to the current page, notesArr is a simple array copy of the page's current notes, and current_index is the index's starting value, which is used as the unique ID for every note.

```
var page;

var notesArr = [];

var current_index = -1;
```

The pageLoaded() Function

Using exports, functions become available in the context of the page. We noticed earlier in the notes-page.xml file that the pageLoaded() method is called when the page is loaded.

```
exports.pageLoaded = function(args) {
   ...
}
```

We'll begin by obtaining a reference to the page within the pageLoaded() method. The form for creating a new note is then shown, and the application settings are queried to retrieve the presently stored data for the new note title and notes.

```
page = args.object;
pageData.set('showForm', true);

var new_note_title = appSettings.
getString('new_note_title');
var notes = appSettings.getString('notes');
```

Next, while remaining within the pageLoaded() method, see if any notes have been saved locally. If not, we generate a series of notes. This array will be the app's default content for new users. If any notes are already stored locally, we convert them to an array and push that data to the observable array.

It's worth noting that before we push the items into the observable array, we check to see whether it's empty. We must do this because utilizing the camera module causes the page's loaded event to be re-executed once an image is picked. This implies that if we aren't cautious, we will add duplicates to the array every time the user uses the camera.

```
if(!notes){
  notes = [
    {
      index: 0,
      title: '100 push ups'
    },
    {
      index: 1,
      title: '100 sit ups'
```

```
      },
      {
        index: 2,
        title: '100 squats'
      },
      {
        index: 3,
        title: '10km running'
      }
    ];
  }else{
    notes = JSON.parse(notes);
  }
  notesArr = notes;
  if(!pageArray.length){
    for(var x = 0; x < notes.length; x++){
      current_index += 1;
      pageArray.push(notes[x]);
    }
  }
}
```

Now that we've added the notes data, we can change the page title by updating the item title property to the value we obtained from the application settings earlier. Then, tie pageData to the page to automatically change the UI anytime we've set changes.

```
pageData.set('item_title', new_note_title);
args.object.bindingContext = pageData;
```

Animate the form for creating new notes. We do this by calling the get-ViewById method in the view and handing in the context (the current page) as the first parameter and the id property associated with the element we wish to change.

Then, call the animate function. This accepts an object holding the animation settings. In this case, we want the form to go down 160 pixels from its initial location over 800 milliseconds.

```
view.getViewById(page, 'form').animate({
    translate: { x: 0, y: 160 },
    duration: 800,
});
```

The newNote() Function

When user taps on the New Item action item in the header, the newNote() method is called. Depending on the current value of showForm, this hides and reveals the new item ListView and slides the form up or down.

If showForm is true, which indicates that it is currently visible, we change the opacity of the ListView to 1 over 400 milliseconds and then slide the form up to conceal it. Otherwise, the ListView is hidden and the form is slid down.

```
exports.newNote = function() {
  var showForm = pageData.get('showForm');
  var top_position = (showForm)?  -160 : 160;
  var list_visibility = (showForm)?  1 : 0;
  view.getViewById(page, 'list').animate({
    opacity: list_visibility,
    duration: 400
  });
  view.getViewById(page, 'form').animate({
      translate: { x: 0, y: top_position },
      duration: 800,
  });
  pageData.set('showForm', !showForm);
}
```

The btnLoaded() Function

We have a loaded property in the button for removing a note in the notes-page.xml file. This is the function that is called when the event occurs.

When a button is created within a ListView item, the function associated to the ListView's itemTap property is not run by default. This is because NativeScript expects that those buttons can only trigger the actions for each list item.

The following code is a workaround for the default behavior. This effectively takes the emphasis off the delete button, allowing continuing to perform a function when a user taps on a ListView item. We don't need this code in this example because we haven't assigned any behavior to item taps, but it's a handy tool to have when working with lists.

```
exports.btnLoaded = function (args) {
  var btn = args.object;
  btn.android.setFocusable(false);
}
```

The openCamera() Function

The next function is openCamera(), which is called when the user presses the Attach Image button. Because the current state is not preserved while utilizing the camera module, we must first store the title of the new note in the application settings.

After that, we can use the takePicture() function to activate the device's default camera app. This function takes an object holding the photo settings as an argument. The promise resolves, and the callback function supplied to then() is run once the user has taken a photo and touched on the Save button in Android or the utilize image button in iOS.

The actual picture is passed to the method as a parameter, and we utilize this to save the file to the document's directory. After that, we store the whole file path and the current app state to the app settings so that we can obtain the value later before storing note.

```
exports.openCamera = function()
{
  appSettings.setString('new_note_title', pageData.
get('itemtitle'));
  cameraModule.takePicture({height: 250,width: 250,
keepAspectRatio: true}).then(function(img)
{
    var filepath = fs.path.join(fs.knownFolders.
documents().path, "img_" + (new Date().getTime() /
1000) + ".jpg");
    img.saveToFile(filepath, uiEnums.ImageFormat.jpeg);
    appSettings.setString('new_note_photo', filepath);
    pageData.set('attachmentimg', filepath);
  });
}
```

The saveNote() Function

When the user presses the Save Note button, the saveNote() method is called. This retrieves the current value of the note title text field and image path, increases the current_index, and inserts the new item into the plain notes and observable notes arrays. Then it stores the current notes and the current_index into the application settings, removes the values for the new note from the application settings, adjusts the UI so that the form is empty, and presents the list while concealing the new note form.

```
exports.saveNote = function() {
  var new_note_title = pageData.get('item_title');
```

```
    var new_note_photo = pageData.get('attachment_img');
    current_index += 1;
    var new_index = current_index;
    var new_item = {
      index: new_index,
      title: new_note_title,
      photo: new_note_photo,
      show_photo: false
    };
    notesArr.push(new_item);
    pageArray.push(new_item);
    appSettings.setString('notes', JSON.
stringify(notesArr));
    appSettings.setNumber('current_index', new_index);
    appSettings.remove('new_note_title');
    appSettings.remove('new_note_photo');
    pageData.set('showForm', false);
    pageData.set('item_title', '');
    pageData.set('attachment_img', null);
    view.getViewById(page, 'list').animate({
      opacity: 1,
      duration: 400
    });

    view.getViewById(page, 'form').animate({
        translate: { x: 0, y: -160 },
        duration: 800,
    });
}
```

The deleteNote() Function

Finally, the deleteNote() method is called when a user hits the remove button within a list item. As seen by previous functions, an object is supplied as an input to functions connected as an event handler for a certain component. The object attribute of this object relates to the component itself.

We may then get the value of an attribute that was passed to it. In this situation, we acquire the index attribute's value and utilize it to determine the actual index of the object we wish to remove.

```
exports.deleteNote = function(args) {
  var target = args.object;
  var index_to_delete = notesArr.map(function(e) {
```

```
      return e.index;
  }).indexOf(target.index);
  notesArr.map(function(item, index){
    if(index == index_to_delete){
      notesArr.splice(index_to_delete, 1);
      pageArray.splice(index_to_delete, 1);
      return false;
    }
  });
  appSettings.setString('notes', JSON.
stringify(notesArr));
}
```

Adding Styles

Add the following global styles to the app.css file:

```
ActionBar {
    background-color: #b898ff;
    color: #fff;
}
.header-item {
    text-transform: uppercase;
}
.item {
    padding: 20;
    font-size: 20px;
}
.form-container {
    background-color: #fff;
    margin-top: -160px;
    padding: 20px;
    z-index: 10;
}
.label {
    font-size: 18px;
}

.link {
    text-align: left;
    background-color: transparent;
    color: #0275d8;
    padding: 5px;
    margin: 10px 0;
```

```
    text-transform: uppercase;
    font-size: 15px;
}
.image {
    width: 300;
    margin: 20 0;
}
.primary-button {
    padding: 5px;
    color: #fff;
    background-color: #0723bb;
    text-transform: uppercase;
}
.delete-button {
    font-size: 15px;
    background-color: #f50029;
    color: #fff;
}
```

We may also create a notes-page.css file and set our styles there to apply page-specific styles.

Running and Debugging the App

We may run the app on our smartphone by typing tns run followed by the platform we wish to deploy. For Android, here's an example:

```
tns run android
```

If the Android platform hasn't already been installed, this will install it for us and then execute the program on our device after it's been installed. Once the app is running, type tns livesync android – watch to automatically refresh whenever we make changes to the source files.

DEBUGGING

NativeScript, like any other app framework, allows developers to debug their program. This is accomplished using the Chrome dev tools. There are two approaches to this:

1. If we already have an app running, open a new terminal window and type tns debug android – start to attach a debugger to the app instance that is already executing.

2. If we don't already have an app running, use tns debug android – debug-brk to create a debugger attached instance of the app.

Whatever choice we select, a new tab in the Google Chrome browser will open, debugging the app just like a regular JavaScript web app. This implies that we can utilize console. Inspect the contents of the variables we're working with by logging into our source code.

LAYOUTS IN NativeScript

The Fundamentals: When developing an app, design for devices of different shapes and sizes must be designed. NativeScript has a variety of layout containers to let us create a versatile UI for any circumstance. NativeScript has very great documentation on their layout containers here, but these applications demonstrate the capabilities.

That app appears to be quite helpful, but we're going to demonstrate the greater potential of layout containers and how we can produce rich UI with basic markup.

By redesigning the layout of a popular app ... the standard weather app on iOS, we'll show how to leverage layouts to create complex UI.

Let's begin by building a small NativeScript Angular app. Open a terminal window and type tns create. The NativeScript CLI will guide us through the available options. Give it a name, select Angular as the flavor, and then select the Hello World template. This creates a basic app with a list of soccer players and a detailed view for each. We'll just delete the items.component.html file and utilize it to build our clone weather app.

The weather view has a panel at the top that displays the location, weather, and temperature. Then there's a part with today's hourly information and the weather forecast for the following seven days.

GridLayout

```
<GridLayout rows="*, auto, auto">
</GridLayout>
```

GridLayout is a layout that generates columns and rows in which additional views can reside. The above HTML defines a GridLayout that will span the entire screen and contain three rows. Because we didn't declare any columns, it will just have one column that takes up the entire screen. The first row (*) takes up the rest of the screen, thus any empty space after the following two rows measures. The following two rows (auto) indicate that the rows will be the height of the content. So, regardless of the device, this app will have a great huge top space for the current weather.

StackLayout

```
<GridLayout rows="*, auto, auto">
  <StackLayout>
    <Label text="Dover"></Label>
    <Label text="Sunny"></Label>
    <Label text="79"></Label>
  </StackLayout>
</GridLayout>
```

The next layout we'll use is StackLayout. This layout just layers views on top of one another. It also contains a property orientation that, when set to horizontal, stacks views left to right. With the markup above, we've generated the first row of our weather app. It may not look great now, but we are using NativeScript layouts to display data in our app, which is quite exciting.

We want the applications I develop to appear beautiful as we go, so let's clean this up a little before we get too far. All of this data is hardcoded, and we'll go over the data layer in another blog to decide what the weather is like. Let's imagine it's 79 degrees and sunny. Our app's backdrop image will indicate the current climate; therefore, choose a good sunny image.

```
<GridLayout rows="*, auto, auto">
  <Image src="https://s7d2.scene7.com/is/image/
TWCNews/1031_nc_sunny_weather_2-1"
iosOverflowSafeArea="true" stretch="aspectFill"
rowSpan="3"></Image>
  <StackLayout>
    <Label text="Dover"></Label>
    <Label text="Cloudy"></Label>
    <Label text="79"></Label>
  </StackLayout>
</GridLayout>
```

An essential feature of GridLayout is the ability to pile views on top of each other. Our image will be shown behind the StackLayout, acting as a backdrop image. We set rowSpan to 3 because we want it to appear beneath all of our content. We set iosOverflowSafeArea to true to have it appear beneath the notch and status bar.

Keep in mind that the first row is now filling up the full screen. Because no new content is added to the following rows, they measure 0 high because they are set to auto, and the * row takes up all available space, in this instance the entire screen.

Another issue we must address is that the StackLayout is taking up the entire screen, with the content at the top. The text should be centered in the row. Such we're going to try something new: we're going to rearrange our rows so that the material in the first row is always in the center.

```
rows="*, auto, *, auto, auto
```

Now we can put our StackLayout with the current weather in the second row so that its height is appropriately measured, and the first and third rows take up the remainder of the available space. As a result, our additional material will now be put in rows 4 and 5.

When stating which row the material should go in when indicating which column the content should go in, the rows start at 0.

```
<GridLayout rows="*, auto *, auto, auto">
  <Image src="https://s7d2.scene7.com/is/image/
TWCNews/1031_nc_sunny_weather_2-1" rowSpan="5"
iosOverflowSafeArea="true" stretch="aspectFill">
</Image>
  <StackLayout row="1">
    <Label text="Dover"></Label>
    <Label text="Sunny"></Label>
    <Label text="79"></Label>
  </StackLayout>
</GridLayout>
```

StackLayout is in row #1, indicating that it belongs in the GridLayout's auto row.

To make it appear lovely, let's add some utility classes and some inline styling. The following helper classes are included in a standard NativeScript app:

```
<GridLayout rows="*, auto *, auto, auto">
  <Image src="https://s7d2.scene7.com/is/image/
TWCNews/1031_nc_sunny_weather_2-1" rowSpan="5"
iosOverflowSafeArea="true" stretch="aspectFill"></Image>
```

```
<StackLayout row="1" class="text-center">
  <Label text="Dover" class="h1" style="color:
white;"></Label>
  <Label text="Sunny" class="h2" style="color:
white;"></Label>
  <Label text="79" class="h1" style="color:
white;"></Label>
  </StackLayout>
</GridLayout>
```

Now, let's put a Label in each of the other rows and watch what happens:

```
<GridLayout rows="*, auto *, auto, auto">
  <Image src="https://s7d2.scene7.com/is/image/
TWCNews/1031_nc_sunny_weather_2-1" rowSpan="5"
iosOverflowSafeArea="true" stretch="aspectFill">
</Image>
  <StackLayout row="1" class="text-center">
    <Label text="Dover" class="h1" style="color:
white;"></Label>
    <Label text="Cloudy" class="h2" style="color:
white;"></Label>
    <Label text="79" class="h1" style="color:
white;"></Label>
  </StackLayout>
  <Label text="Hourly data goes here" row="3">
</Label>
  <Label text="7 day forecast goes here" row="4">
</Label>
</GridLayout>
```

ScrollView

ScrollView is not a layout, but it is a view that we will frequently use in our layouts. To produce this view, we'll combine ScrollView with a horizontally oriented StackLayout:

```
<GridLayout rows="*, auto *, auto, auto">
  <Image src="https://s7d2.scene7.com/is/image/
TWCNews/1031_nc_sunny_weather_2-1" rowSpan="5"
iosOverflowSafeArea="true" stretch="aspectFill">
</Image>
  <StackLayout row="1" class="text-center">
```

```
    <Label text="Dover" class="h2" style="color:
white;"></Label>
    <Label text="Cloudy" class="h3" style="color:
white;"></Label>
    <Label text="79" class="h1" style="color:
white;"></Label>
  </StackLayout>
  <ScrollView row="3" orientation="horizontal">
    <StackLayout orientation="horizontal">
      <StackLayout style="color: white; margin: 10;
font-size: 13;" class="text-center">
        <Label text="Now"></Label>
        <Image src="https://cdn.pixabay.com/
photo/2015/12/03/15/43/sun-1075154_960_720.png"
height="20" margin="5"></Image>
        <Label text="79"></Label>
      </StackLayout>
      <StackLayout style="color: white; margin: 10;
font-size: 13;" class="text-center">
        <Label text="10am"></Label>
        <Image src="https://cdn.pixabay.com/
photo/2015/12/03/15/43/sun-1075154_960_720.png"
height="20" margin="5"></Image>
        <Label text="81"></Label>
      </StackLayout>
    </StackLayout>
  </ScrollView>
  <Label text="7 day forecase goes here" margin="50"
row="4"></Label>
</GridLayout>
```

It's worth noting that we've designated the ScrollView as the view that will occupy row #3. Because ScrollView can only have one immediate child, we use it as our horizontal StackLayout and then add a few of StackLayouts to represent the time, weather icon, and temperature. To test the ScrollView, we are going to duplicate a large number of the StackLayouts in the horizontal StackLayout.

Rows 0 and 2 take up the rest of the available space.

We are going to hardcode the data because this blog is only about layouts. Of course, this isn't how an app like this would function; the hourly data would be delivered by an API as an array and bound to the display, but that's a topic for another article. For the time being, we'll create a UI mockup using hardcoded HTML.

We failed to include the High and Low bar directly above the horizontal hourly scroller, so let's do that now. We'll need to restructure a little, but we can just put everything in a StackLayout and add it to the row where the scroller is. Row 3 becomes as follows:

```
<StackLayout row="3">
  <GridLayout columns="auto, *, auto, auto"
style="color: white; border-bottom-width: 1; border-
bottom-color: rgba(255,255,255,0.2)">
    <Label text="Friday" class="m-x-10 m-b-10"></
Label>
    <Label text="TODAY" col="1" class="m-x-10 m-b-
10"></Label>
    <Label text="91" col="2" class="m-x-10 m-b-10"></
Label>
    <Label text="65" col="3" class="m-x-10 m-b-10"
opacity=".5"></Label>
  </GridLayout>
  <ScrollView orientation="horizontal">
    <StackLayout orientation="horizontal">
      <StackLayout style="color: white; margin: 10;
font-size: 13;" class="text-center">
        <Label text="Now"></Label>
        <Image src="https://cdn.pixabay.com/
photo/2015/12/03/15/43/sun-1075154_960_720.png"
height="20" margin="5"></Image>
        <Label text="79"></Label>
      </StackLayout>
      <!--...repeated hourly views go here.-->
    </StackLayout>
  </ScrollView>
</StackLayout>
```

For the bar above the hourly scroller, we utilized a GridLayout. Important: If we do not specify a row or col for a view in the GridLayout, it will be put in row 0.

We utilized the helper classes m-x-10 for horizontal margins and m-b-10 for margin bottoms.

We'll use GridLayout again to build those rows in the same way we did before:

```
<GridLayout rows="auto" columns="auto, *, auto, auto">
  <Label text="Saturday" class="m-x-10 m-b-10"></
Label>
  <Image col="1" src="https://cdn.pixabay.com/
photo/2015/12/03/15/43/sun-1075154_960_720.png"
height="20" margin="5"></Image>
  <Label col="2" text="88" class="m-x-10"></Label>
  <Label col="3" text="66" class="m-x-10"
opacity=".5"></Label>
</GridLayout>
```

UI LAYOUT CONTAINERS

AbsoluteLayout

The AbsoluteLayout is NativeScript's most basic layout. It positions its children using absolute left-top coordinates. When the size of the AbsoluteLayout changes, it will not impose any layout restrictions on its children and will not resize them at runtime.

AbsoluteLayout Child Properties

Property	Description
Left	The pixel distance between the child's left edge and the left edge of its parent AbsoluteLayout client area is get or set.
Top	Gets or sets the pixel distance between the child's top edge and the top edge of its parent AbsoluteLayout client area.

First Source Code:

```
<Page xmlns="http://schemas.nativescript.org/tns.xsd">
 <AbsoluteLayout width="200" height="200"
backgroundColor="lightgray">
   <Label text="11, 10" left="10" top="10" width="80"
height="80" backgroundColor="red"/>
   <Label text="100, 10" left="110" top="10"
width="80" height="80" backgroundColor="green"/>
   <Label text="100, 110" left="110" top="110"
width="80" height="80" backgroundColor="blue"/>
   <Label text="11, 110" left="10" top="110"
width="80" height="80" backgroundColor="yellow"/>
```

```
  </AbsoluteLayout>
</Page>
```

Second Source Code:

```
<Page xmlns="http://schemas.nativescript.org/tns.xsd">
  <AbsoluteLayout width="200" height="200"
backgroundColor="lightgray">
    <Label text="no margin" left="9" top="9"
width="100" height="100" backgroundColor="red"/>
    <Label text="margin='30'" left="9" top="9"
margin="30" width="100" height="90"
backgroundColor="green"/>
  </AbsoluteLayout>
</Page>
```

DockLayout

The DockLayout is a layout that allows child components to dock to the left, right, top, bottom, or center of the layout. Use the dock attribute of a child element to define its docking side. To dock a child element to the DockLayout's center, it must be the DockLayout's final child and have the stretchLastChild property set to true.

DockLayout Properties
PROPERTY
DESCRIPTION

stretchLastChild
Gets or sets a value that indicates whether the final child element in a DockLayout grows to fill the available space. The default value is true.

DockLayout Child Properties

Property	Description
Dock	This property specifies the Dock location of a child element included within a DockLayout. There are four possible values: left, top, right, and bottom.

stretchLastChild="false" example:

```
<Page xmlns="http://schemas.nativescript.org/tns.xsd">
  <DockLayout width="200" height="200"
backgroundColor="lightgray" stretchLastChild="false">
```

```
    <Label text="left" dock="left" width="50"
backgroundColor="green"/>
    <Label text="top" dock="top" height="50"
backgroundColor="blue"/>
    <Label text="right" dock="right" width="50"
backgroundColor="yellow"/>
    <Label text="bottom" dock="bottom" height="50"
backgroundColor="red"/>
  </DockLayout>
</Page>
```

stretchLastChild= "true" example:

```
<Page xmlns="http://schemas.nativescript.org/tns.
xsd">
  <DockLayout width="200" height="200"
backgroundColor="lightgray" stretchLastChild="true">
    <Label text="left" dock="left"
backgroundColor="green"/>
    <Label text="top" dock="top"
backgroundColor="blue"/>
    <Label text="right" dock="right" backgroundColor=
" yellow "/>
    <Label text="bottom" dock="bottom"
backgroundColor="red"/>
  </DockLayout>
</Page>
```

Multiple child elements on one side example:

```
<Page xmlns="http://schemas.nativescript.org/tns.xsd">
  <DockLayout width="200" height="200"
backgroundColor="lightgray" stretchLastChild="true">
    <Label text="left1" dock="left"
backgroundColor="green"/>
    <Label text="left2" dock="left"
backgroundColor="blue"/>
    <Label text="left3" dock="left"
backgroundColor="yellow"/>
    <Label text="last child" backgroundColor="red"/>
  </DockLayout>
</Page>
```

The GridLayout

The GridLayout is a layout that organizes its child objects into rows and columns in a table. A cell can have several child components; they can span multiple rows and columns, and even overlap. By default, the GridLayout has one column and one row. To add more columns and rows, provide column definition items (separated by commas) in the GridLayout's columns property and row definition items (separated by commas) in the GridLayout's rows property. The width and height of a column and row can be provided as an absolute number of pixels, as a percentage of available space, or automatically:

- **Absolute:** Pixels have a fixed size.

- **Star (*):** Uses all available space (after filling all auto and fixed sized columns), proportionately split among all star-sized columns. So 3/7 is equivalent to 30/70.

- **Auto:** Uses as much space as the enclosed child element(s) requires.

GridLayout Properties

Property	Description
Columns	A comma-separated text value indicates column widths. Column widths can be specified as an exact number, an auto value, or a *. A number represents the absolute column width, auto makes the column the width of its widest child, and * makes the column take up all available horizontal space.
Rows	A string value bounded by commas represents row heights. Row heights can be specified as an absolute number, an auto value, or a *. A number denotes the absolute row height, auto makes the row as tall as its highest kid, and * makes the row take up all available vertical space.

GridLayout Child Properties

Property	Description
Row	Gets or sets a value indicating which row child content inside a GridLayout should be shown.
Column	Gets or sets a value indicating which column child content inside a GridLayout should be shown.
rowSpan	Gets or sets a value indicating the total number of rows spanned by child content within a GridLayout.
colSpan	Gets or sets a value indicating the total number of columns spanned by child content inside a GridLayout.

A simple Grid use example:

```
<Page xmlns="http://schemas.nativescript.org/tns.xsd">
  <GridLayout columns="40, auto, *" rows="50, auto, *"
width="200" height="200" backgroundColor="lightgray" >
    <Label text="Label 1" row="0" col="0"
backgroundColor="yellow"/>
    <Label text="Label 2" row="0" col="1" colSpan="2"
backgroundColor="purple"/>
    <Label text="Label 3" row="1" col="0" rowSpan="2"
backgroundColor="green"/>
    <Label text="Label 4" row="1" col="1"
backgroundColor="orange"/>
    <Label text="Label 5" row="1" col="2"
backgroundColor="green"/>
    <Label text="Label 6" row="2" col="1"
backgroundColor="yellow"/>
    <Label text="Label 7" row="2" col="2"
backgroundColor="pink"/>
  </GridLayout>
</Page>
```

Sizing with a star (*) example:

```
<Page xmlns="http://schemas.nativescript.org/tns.xsd">
  <GridLayout columns="*,2*" rows="2*,3*" width="250"
height="250" backgroundColor="lightgray" >
    <Label text="Label 1" col="0" row="0"
backgroundColor="yellow"/>
    <Label text="Label 2" col="1" row="0"
backgroundColor="blue"/>
    <Label text="Label 3" col="0" row="1"
backgroundColor="red"/>
    <Label text="Label 4" col="1" row="1"
backgroundColor="green"/>
  </GridLayout>
</Page>
```

Fixed and auto sizing example:

```
<Page xmlns="http://schemas.nativescript.org/tns.xsd">
  <GridLayout columns="90,auto" rows="90,auto"
width="200" height="200" backgroundColor="lightgray" >
    <Label text="Label 1" col="0" row="0"
backgroundColor="green"/>
```

```
    <Label text="Label 2" col="1" row="0"
backgroundColor="blue"/>
    <Label text="Label 3" col="0" row="1"
backgroundColor="yellow"/>
    <Label text="Label 4" col="1" row="1"
backgroundColor="red"/>
  </GridLayout>
</Page>
```

For no width and horizontalAlignment!= stretch, consider the following example. The star columns will not occupy the complete available area if the GridLayout has no explicit width specified and its horizontalAlignment is set but not extend (200 from parent StackLayout).

```
<Page xmlns="http://schemas.nativescript.org/tns.xsd">
  <StackLayout width="210" height="210"
backgroundColor="palegreen">
    <GridLayout columns="*,2*"
horizontalAlignment="right" verticalAlignment="top"
backgroundColor="gray">
      <Label text="Label 1" col="0"
backgroundColor="green"/>
      <Label text="Label 2" col="1"
backgroundColor="red"/>
    </GridLayout>
  </StackLayout>
</Page>
```

Label 3 has a set width of 150 pixels as an example of column stretching. Because Label 3 stretches the auto column, Label 1 is given more space than it requires.

```
<Page xmlns="http://schemas.nativescript.org/
tns.xsd">
  <GridLayout columns="auto,100" rows="auto,auto"
width="240" height="240" backgroundColor="lightgray" >
    <Label text="Label 1" col="0" row="0"
backgroundColor="green"/>
    <Label text="Label 2" col="1" row="0"
backgroundColor="blue"/>
```

```
    <Label text="Label 3" width="150" col="0" row="1"
backgroundColor="red"/>
  </GridLayout>
</Page>
```

Exemplification of a Complex Structure: The image has a set width and height of 72 pixels and spans both rows. The first Label is given additional space by setting colSpan="2." Because the fourth Label extends the auto column, the third Label is given more space than required.

```
<Page xmlns="http://schemas.nativescript.org/tns.xsd">
  <GridLayout columns="auto, *, auto" rows="auto, 25"
verticalAlignment="top" backgroundColor="gray">
    <Image src="~/cute.jpg" rowSpan="2" width="71"
height="72" margin="3" verticalAlignment="top"/>
    <Label text="My cat loves camera" textWrap="true"
col="1" colSpan="2" minHeight="40" fontSize="25"
margin="3"/>
    <Label text="John-Smith" col="1" row="1"
fontSize="12" horizontalAlignment="left"
verticalAlignment="bottom" margin="3"/>
    <Label text="comments: 26" col="2" row="1"
color="green" fontSize="13" verticalAlignment="bottom"
margin="3"/>
  </GridLayout>
</Page>
```

StackLayout

Depending on its orientation, the StackLayout stacks its child elements below or beside each other. Making lists is quite beneficial.

StackLayout Properties

Property	Description
Orientation	Gets or sets whether the child items should be stacked horizontally or vertically. Vertical and horizontal values are both possible. Vertical is the default setting.

StackLayout Child Properties

As an example of orientation="vertical,":

```
<Page xmlns="http://schemas.nativescript.org/tns.xsd">
  <StackLayout orientation="vertical" width="200"
height="200" backgroundColor="lightgray">
```

```
    <Label text="Label 1" width="40" height="40"
backgroundColor="green"/>
    <Label text="Label 2" width="40" height="40"
backgroundColor="yellow"/>
    <Label text="Label 3" width="40" height="40"
backgroundColor="red"/>
    <Label text="Label 4" width="40" height="40"
backgroundColor="blue"/>
  </StackLayout>
</Page>
```

As an example of orientation= "horizontal,":

```
<Page xmlns="http://schemas.nativescript.org/tns.xsd">
  <StackLayout orientation="horizontal" width="200"
height="200" backgroundColor="lightgray">
    <Label text="Label 1" width="40" height="40"
backgroundColor="yellow"/>
    <Label text="Label 2" width="40" height="40"
backgroundColor="blue"/>
    <Label text="Label 3" width="40" height="40"
backgroundColor="green"/>
    <Label text="Label 4" width="40" height="40"
backgroundColor="red"/>
  </StackLayout>
</Page>
```

As an example, consider the horizontal alignment of children:

```
<Page xmlns="http://schemas.nativescript.org/tns.xsd">
  <StackLayout orientation="vertical" width="200"
height="200" backgroundColor="lightgray">
    <Label text="Label 1" horizontalAlignment="left"
backgroundColor="yellow"/>
    <Label text="Label 2" horizontalAlignment="center"
backgroundColor="blue"/>
    <Label text="Label 3" horizontalAlignment="right"
backgroundColor="green"/>
    <Label text="Label 4"
horizontalAlignment="stretch" backgroundColor="red"/>
  </StackLayout>
</Page>
```

As an illustration, consider the vertical alignment of children:

```
<Page xmlns="http://schemas.nativescript.org/tns.xsd">
  <StackLayout orientation="horizontal" width="200"
height="200" backgroundColor="lightgray">
    <Label text="Label 1" verticalAlignment="top"
backgroundColor="green"/>
    <Label text="Label 2" verticalAlignment="center"
backgroundColor="blue"/>
    <Label text="Label 3" verticalAlignment="bottom"
backgroundColor="yellow"/>
    <Label text="Label 4" verticalAlignment="stretch"
backgroundColor="red"/>
  </StackLayout>
</Page>
```

WrapLayout

The WrapLayout is similar to the StackLayout in that it stacks all child components to one column/row, but it also wraps them to additional columns/rows if there is no space left. The WrapLayout is frequently used with elements of the same size, but this is not required.

WrapLayout Properties

Property	Description
Orientation	This function returns or sets a value representing the flow direction. Items are grouped in rows when the orientation is horizontal. Items are placed in columns when the orientation is vertical. The horizontal setting is the default.
itemWidth	The width used to layout and measure each child is returned or set. The default value is Number.NaN, which does not limit the number of children.
itemHeight	This method returns or sets the height used to measure and layout each child. The default value is Number.NaN, which does not limit the number of children.

WrapLayout Child Properties

Example of "horizontal" orientation:

```
<Page xmlns="http://schemas.nativescript.org/tns.xsd">
  <WrapLayout orientation="horizontal" width="200"
height="200" backgroundColor="lightgray">
```

```
    <Label text="Label 1" width="60" height="60"
backgroundColor="green"/>
    <Label text="Label 2" width="60" height="60"
backgroundColor="blue"/>
    <Label text="Label 3" width="60" height="60"
backgroundColor="yellow"/>
    <Label text="Label 4" width="60" height="60"
backgroundColor="red"/>
  </WrapLayout>
</Page>
```

Example of orientation="vertical,":

```
<Page xmlns="http://schemas.nativescript.org/tns.xsd">
  <WrapLayout orientation="vertical" width="200"
height="200" backgroundColor="lightgray">
    <Label text="Label 1" width="60" height="60"
backgroundColor="green"/>
    <Label text="Label 2" width="60" height="60"
backgroundColor="blue"/>
    <Label text="Label 3" width="60" height="60"
backgroundColor="yellow"/>
    <Label text="Label 4" width="60" height="60"
backgroundColor="red"/>
  </WrapLayout>
</Page>
```

For instance, itemWidth="30" and itemHeight="30":

```
<Page xmlns="http://schemas.nativescript.org/tns.xsd">
  <WrapLayout itemWidth="30" itemHeight="30"
width="200" height="200" backgroundColor="lightgray">
    <Label text="Label 1" width="60" height="60"
backgroundColor="green"/>
    <Label text="Label 2" width="60" height="60"
backgroundColor="blue"/>
    <Label text="Label 3" width="60" height="60"
backgroundColor="yellow"/>
    <Label text="Label 4" width="60" height="60"
backgroundColor="red"/>
  </WrapLayout>
</Page>
```

FlexboxLayout

The FlexboxLayout is a non-conforming CSS Flexible Box Layout implementation based on an existing Apache-2 licensed flexbox implementation provided at github.com/google/flexbox-layout.

FlexboxLayout Properties

Property	Description	Values
flexDirection	Gets or sets a value specifying the orientation of flex items in the flex container.	• row (the same as text direction) is the default. • row reversal (opposite to text direction). • a column (same as row but top to bottom). • column reversal (same as the row-reverse top to bottom).
flexWrap	Gets or sets a value indicating whether the flex elements must be on a single line or flowing into multiple lines. If it is set to many lines, it also sets the cross-axis, which dictates the direction in which new lines are piled.	• default nowrap (single-line, which may cause the container to overflow). • wrap (multilines, direction is defined by flexDirection). • reverse-wrap (multilines, opposite to direction defined by flexDirection).
justifyContent	This method returns or sets a value showing the alignment along the main axis. It aids in distributing extra free space when all of the flex items on a line are either inflexible or have reached their maximum size. It also has some influence over the alignment of items that overflow the line.	• flex-start (items are packed closer to the start line) is the default. • flexible-end (items are packed toward end line). • the center (items are centered along line). • space-between (The items in the line are uniformly distributed; the first item is on the start line, and the last item is on the finish line.). • space-around (The objects on the line are uniformly spaced, with equal space surrounding them.).
alignItems	Gets or sets a value specifying how flex items on the current line are laid out along the cross axis. Consider it the justifyContent variant for the cross-axis (perpendicular to the main-axis).	• flex start (The items' cross-start margin edge is put on the cross-start line.). • flex-end (The items' cross-end margin edge is positioned on the cross-end line.). • the center (The cross-axis is centered on the items.). • baseline (Items are aligned in the notion that their baselines are aligned.). • stretch (extend to fill the container while keeping the min/max widths in mind) default.

(Continued)

Property	Description	Values
alignContent	Gets or sets a value that aids in aligning the lines within a flex container when there is additional space in the cross-axis, in the same way that justifyContent aligns individual items inside the main-axis.	• flex start (lines packed to the container's beginning). • flex-end (lines packed to the container's end). • the center (lines packed to the container's center). • space-between (lines are distributed uniformly; the first line begins at the beginning of the container and the final one ends at the end). • space-around (lines that are distributed uniformly and have equal space between them). • stretch (lines stretch to fill the remaining space). When the flexbox has simply a single line, this attribute has no impact.

FlexboxLayout Child Properties

Property	Description
Order	This property returns or sets a value that alters the default ordering of flex components.
flexGrow	Gets or sets a unitless number that acts as a percentage to indicate if the flex item can increase if necessary. It specifies how much space the item should take up inside the flex container.
flexShrink	Gets or sets a value showing the "flex shrink factor," which defines how much the flex item shrinks in comparison to the rest of the flex items in the flex container when there is insufficient space on the row. When it is missing, it is set to 1, and when distributing negative space, the flex shrink factor is increased by the flex basis.
alignSelf	Gets or sets a value that allows the alignItems value for certain flex items to be overridden. This property accepts the same five values as alignItems: flex-start (cross-start margin edge of the item is placed on the cross-start line), flex-end (cross-end margin edge of the item is placed on the cross-end line), center (item is centered in the cross-axis), baseline (items are aligned such that their baseline is aligned), and stretch (stretch to fill the container but still respect min-width). The default setting is stretch.
flexWrapBefore	Gets or sets the boolean value that controls item wrapping. When we set it to true on a flexbox item, it will compel it to wrap on a new line. The value false is the default. This attribute is not included in the flexbox definition.

FlexDirection="row" and alignItems="stretch" (default) example:

```
<Page xmlns="http://schemas.nativescript.org/tns.xsd">
  <FlexboxLayout width="250" height="250"
backgroundColor="lightgray">
    <Label text="Label 1" width="60" height="60"
backgroundColor="yellow"/>
    <Label text="Label 2" width="60" height="60"
backgroundColor="blue"/>
    <Label text="Label 3" width="60" height="60"
backgroundColor="green"/>
    <Label text="Label 4" width="60" height="60"
backgroundColor="red"/>
  </FlexboxLayout>
</Page>
```

FlexDirection="column" and alignItems="stretch" (default) example:

```
<Page xmlns="http://schemas.nativescript.org/tns.xsd">
  <FlexboxLayout flexDirection="column" width="250"
height="250" backgroundColor="lightgray">
    <Label text="Label 1" width="60" height="60"
backgroundColor="green"/>
    <Label text="Label 2" width="60" height="60"
backgroundColor="blue"/>
    <Label text="Label 3" width="60" height="60"
backgroundColor="yellow"/>
    <Label text="Label 4" width="60" height="60"
backgroundColor="red"/>
  </FlexboxLayout>
</Page>
```

flexDirection="row" and alignItems="flex-start" example:

```
<Page xmlns="http://schemas.nativescript.org/tns.xsd">
  <FlexboxLayout alignItems="flex-start" width="250"
height="250" backgroundColor="lightgray">
    <Label text="Label 1" width="60" height="60"
backgroundColor="green"/>
    <Label text="Label 2" width="60" height="60"
backgroundColor="blue"/>
    <Label text="Label 3" width="60" height="60"
backgroundColor="yellow"/>
```

```
    <Label text="Label 4" width="60" height="60"
backgroundColor="red"/>
    </FlexboxLayout>
</Page>
```

flexDirection="row", custom order example:

```
<Page xmlns="http://schemas.nativescript.org/tns.xsd">
  <FlexboxLayout alignItems="flex-start" width="250"
height="250" backgroundColor="lightgray">
    <Label order="3" text="Label 1" width="60"
height="60" backgroundColor="green"/>
    <Label order="4" text="Label 2" width="60"
height="60" backgroundColor="blue"/>
    <Label order="2" text="Label 3" width="60"
height="60" backgroundColor="yellow"/>
    <Label order="1" text="Label 4" width="60"
height="60" backgroundColor="red"/>
  </FlexboxLayout>
</Page>
```

flexWrap= "wrap" example:

```
<Page xmlns="http://schemas.nativescript.org/tns.xsd">
  <FlexboxLayout flexWrap="wrap" height="250"
width="250" backgroundColor="lightgray">
    <Label text="Label 1" width="90" height="50"
backgroundColor="blue"/>
    <Label text="Label 2" width="90" height="50"
backgroundColor="yellow"/>
    <Label text="Label 3" width="90" height="50"
backgroundColor="red"/>
    <Label text="Label 4" width="90" height="50"
backgroundColor="green"/>
  </FlexboxLayout>
</Page>
```

flexDirection="column-reverse", justifyContent="space-around" and alignItems="stretch" example:

```
<Page xmlns="http://schemas.nativescript.org/tns.xsd">
  <FlexboxLayout flexDirection="column-reverse"
justifyContent="space-around" alignItems="stretch"
```

```
    height="300" width="300" backgroundColor="white">
    <Label text="Label 1" width="40" height="40"
backgroundColor="red"/>
    <Label alignSelf="center" text="Label 2"
width="40" height="40" backgroundColor="lightgray"/>
    <Label alignSelf="flex-end" text="Label 3"
width="40" height="40" backgroundColor="yellow"/>
    <Label text="Label 4" width="40" height="40"
backgroundColor="blue"/>
  </FlexboxLayout>
</Page>
```

In this chapter, we discussed the structure of an application in NativeScript and page navigation. We also talked about the basic layout and its many forms through examples.

CHAPTER 3

Refining Your App

IN THIS CHAPTER

➤ Working with data

➤ Native hardware

➤ Deploying an Android app

➤ Preparing an iOS app for distribution

➤ iOS security and building our app with Xcode

In the last chapter, we discussed the app's structure, including navigation pages and the app's layout. This chapter discusses dealing with data, native hardware, enhancing user experience, deploying an Android app, and preparing an iOS app.

EIGHT STEPS FOR LAUNCHING OUR NativeScript APP INTO APP STORES

This section contains a step-by-step guide for submitting a NativeScript-built app to the iOS App Store and Google Play.

- **Step 1:** Design our app's icons.

- **Step 2:** Create our splash screens.

- **Step 3:** Set up our metadata.

- **Step 4 (optional):** Install Webpack.

DOI: 10.1201/9781003299394-3

- **Step 5:** Create an Android release build.

- **Step 6:** Google Play.

- **Step 7:** Create an iOS release build.

- **Step 8:** Connect to iTunes.

Step 1: Design Our App Icons

The icon of our app is the first thing customers notice about it. When we create a new NativeScript app, we are given a placeholder icon, which is OK for development, but we must change the placeholder icon with the image we want to use in the stores for production.

To receive our production-ready app icon files, first, generate a 1024 × 1024 pixel.png image asset that symbolizes our app. As an example, here's the graphic we used for Pokémon Types.

If we deal with designers, this is the point at which we should ask them to generate the final picture file for us. There are a few websites that can assist us if we do not deal with expert designers. For example, we purchased the Pokémon Types icon from VectorStock, which sells high-quality graphic assets for a few bucks.

VectorStock is one of several websites that provide high-quality picture files that may be used as icons for a reasonable fee.

To make matters harder, both iOS and Android demand that we supply a wide range of icon pictures in several sizes. But don't panic; once we have a 1024 × 1024 image, a few websites will produce photos in the different sizes that Android and iOS demand. We propose the Brosteins' superb NativeScript Image Builder, accessible at nsimage.brosteins.com, for NativeScript development.

Visit the website, locate the "Upload an Icon" box, choose a freshly created. png file, and select the "Upload App Icon" button.

How to utilize the NativeScript Image Builder to generate the icon files required for our iOS and Android apps.

When the Image Builder is finished, we'll be prompted to download an icons.zip file. This download includes Android and iOS files containing the image assets we require.

To place those images, begin by accessing our app's app/App Resources/iOS/Assets.xcassets/AppIcon.appiconset folder. The NativeScript placeholder graphics for iOS may be found in this folder. Delete the whole contents of this folder and replace them with the files from our icons.zip download in the iOS folder.

How to use the NativeScript Image Builder to replace the default NativeScript icon images with our image files.

After adding these new pictures, run our NativeScript app on iOS to confirm the new icons appear good. On the iOS simulator, the Pokémon Types icon looks like this.

TIP: Both iOS and Android cache these icon files to save our time during development. If the icon changes do not appear, run tns platform remove ios to delete any current native iOS files. Then, using tns run ios, relaunch our app with our new image assets in place.

Now that we've finished our iOS icons let's move on to Android. To make matters worse, Android has an entirely distinct set of protocols for dealing with icons. (By the way, different processes for iOS and Android are a frequent topic in this section, so we're prepared.)

There is one more significant distinction we should be aware of before creating our Android images. Almost all app icons on iOS have solid color backgrounds. To blend in with other iOS icons, my Pokémon Types icon graphic has a solid white background.

The backgrounds of iOS icons are often solid colors.

On Android, though, icons often have a translucent backdrop. As a result, my Pokémon Types icon has a translucent background to blend in with other Android icons.

The backgrounds of Android icons are often translucent.

That means we should upload two separate 1024 × 1024 pictures to the NativeScript Image Builder, one with a solid background color for iOS and one with a transparent background for Android. That's exactly what I did with Pokémon Types.

Whatever design option we make, open our app's app/App Resources/Android folder once we have our picture assets ready for Android.

Then, copy the icon.png files from our icons.zip file's Android folder and place them in the app/App Resources/Android folder.

How to use the NativeScript Image Builder to replace the default NativeScript Android icon pictures with our image files.

After installing these files, launch our app on Android to confirm that our updated icons appear as expected.

Step 2: Create Our Splash Screens

Splash screens are what users view when they launch our app before it is ready to use. For example, when a user opens Pokémon Types on iOS, this is what they see.

Although a splash screen may be used for various purposes, most apps display the app's logo and possibly the app's logo. NativeScript has a set of standards to make creating this type of splash screen for iOS and Android reasonably simple.

Let's begin with iOS. Open the app/App_Resources/Assets.xcassets folder in our app and look for two folders entitled LaunchScreen. AspectFill.imageset and LaunchScreen.Center.imageset.

These are the default splash screens that we've used in our app up to this point. The AspectFill images serve as the backdrop for our splash screen, and the Center images are centered on top of the background. Assuming we desire a straightforward splash screen, our objective is to alter the background color of the AspectFill photos and insert our logo into the Center images.

At this stage, launch our iOS app to ensure that our updated splash screen files are operating properly.

Once we've completed our iOS setup, we're ready to go on to Android, where our instructions are practically identical this time. A sequence of background.png and logo.png files may be found in our app's app/App_Resources/Android folder. NativeScript, like iOS, utilizes the background.png file as the splash screen's backdrop and centers the logo.png file on top of it. We can use the relevant files under Pokémon Types as a guide, but this step is simply additional image altering.

When we're finished, launch our app on Android to ensure everything is in order and then proceed to configure our app's metadata.

Step 3: Set Up Our Metadata

Before deploying our apps to their separate stores, we must set up a lot of information in iOS and Android applications. Many of these settings have intelligent defaults in NativeScript, but there are a few we should double-check before deploying.

Application id

Our application id is a one-of-a-kind identifier for our app that uses reverse domain name notation. Pokémon Types, for example, has the application id com.tjvantoll.pokemontypereference. The NativeScript CLI includes a standard for specifying the application id during app creation, tns build MyApp – appid com.mycompany.myappname, but it's simple to alter our app id if we didn't use that option.

Locate the "nativescript" key in our app's base package.json file. Check that the "id" property has the value we want to use.

```
{
  "nativescript": {
    "id": "com.tjvantoll.pokemontypereference",
    "tns-android": {
      "version": "2.5.0"
    },
    "tns-ios": {
      "version": "2.5.0"
    }
  },
  ......
}
```

Note: If we update our application id in our package.json file, we may also need to modify the value in our app/App Resources/Android/app.gradle file (look for the applicationId key) for the change to be effective on Android.

Display Name

The display name of our app is the name that appears next to our icon on the user's screen.

Our app's display name appears next to its icon.

NativeScript, by default, determines our app's display name depending on the value we gave to tns create, which is frequently not what we want the user to see. Running tns create pokemon-types, for example, produces an app with the display name "pokemontypes."

To alter that value on iOS, enter the app/App Resources/iOS/Info.plist file in our app. The Info.plist file is the configuration file for iOS, and it contains a variety of parameters that we may wish to experiment with before launching our app. We'll want to change the CFBundleDisplayName value for the display name. This is how this value appears for Pokémon Types.

```
<key>CFBundleDisplayName</key>
<string>PokéTypes</string>
```

One thing to keep in mind: while there is no true character restriction for display names, both iOS and Android will truncate them after about 10–12 characters. For example, when I tried to use "Pokémon Types" as my app's display name, we got the truncated display.

Long display names are truncated by iOS and Android. In this case, iOS is truncating the display name "Pokémon Types."

Because the shortened display is less than ideal, we may need to be creative when naming our program.

The procedure for updating our display name on Android is identical. Look for a file called app/App Resources/Android/values/strings.xml in our app. If the file does not already exist (it does not by default), create it and put in the following code.

```
<?xml version="1.0" encoding="utf-8"?>
<resources>
    <string name="app_name">PokéTypes</string>
    <string name="title_activity_kimera">PokéTypes
</string>
</resources>
```

Then, replace the two "PokéTypes" references with the display name of our app. After we've finished, re-run our app on Android to ensure everything is in order.

Other Metadata

Although the application id and display name are the two most popular choices, there are a few more that we should look at before deploying our app.

We may alter additional settings in our app's app/App Resources/iOS/Info.plist file, such as our app's supported orientations.

On Android, extra configuration variables may be found in the app/App Resources/Android/AndroidManifest.xml file. One thing to look is the permissions we're presently seeking and if they're current with the status of our app.

Finally, our Info.plist and AndroidManifest.xml files include our app's version numbers, which NativeScript defaults to 1.0. If we want to modify those settings, or if we need to update them for an app update, consult the NativeScript instructions on versioning here for iOS and here for Android.

When we're happy with our settings and are ready to begin, let's move on to optimizing our code.

Step 4 (Optional): Install Webpack

NativeScript's source code contains JavaScript, and just like JavaScript code on the web, we may want to optimize it before pushing it to production. Webpack, which NativeScript has built-in support for, is the optimization tool of choice for NativeScript projects.

Before we begin, it's important to note that webpack use is optional for NativeScript projects. Because webpack minimizes the amount of JavaScript code in our app, it will load faster and have a reduced app size when published to app stores.

The amount of value you get using webpack is determined by the app we're creating, most notably its present size.

The drawback of utilizing webpack with NativeScript is that now we have another item to configure and manage. Although NativeScript's webpack plugin is simple to install and use, it might be not easy to customize for advanced use, particularly if we've never used webpack previously. If the deployment processes in this post have already overwhelmed us, we may try publishing our applications to the stores as a first step and then optimizing those apps with webpack in a later release.

It's entirely up to us, but if we want to give webpack a chance, browse over the NativeScript webpack docs. If we run into problems, consider posting a question in the NativeScript community forum.

Let's get started on constructing our apps now that we're all set.

Step 5: Create an Android Release Build

Now that we've completed all of our settings, we're ready to build our app and submit it to the app stores. Let's begin with Android because getting our app into Google Play is much easier than working with the iOS App Store.

Before proceeding to Google Play to register and publish our app (the next step), we must first create an Android executable file for your application. This file has an .apk extension on Android and may be generated with the NativeScript CLI.

The tns run command we've been using during NativeScript development creates an .apk file for us and downloads it on an Android emulator or device. However, the build required for a genuine Google Play release must also be code signed. If we want to get into the cryptographic intricacies, we may refer to Android's code signing instructions, but we need to accomplish two things to build a release version of our Android app.

- Make a file with the extension .keystore or .jks (Java keystore).

- During a build, use that .keystore or .jks file to sign our program.

The Android manual provides several alternatives for creating our keystore file. Our favourite method is to use the keytool command-line software, which is included with the Java JDK on which NativeScript is based and should be available on our development machine's command line.

To use keytool to build a keystore for code signing, run the following command, replacing tj-vantoll with our name or the name of our firm and NameOfYourApp with the name of our app.

- keytool -genkey -v -keystore tj-vantoll.jks -keyalg RSA

- -keysize 2048 -validity 10000 -alias NameOfYourApp

The keytool software will prompt various questions, some of which are optional (such as the name of our company and the names of our city/state/country). Still, the most critical are the passwords for both the keystore and the alias (more on that momentarily). Here's how the keytool process looks when I build the keystore for Pokémon Types.

Before we get into how to use this .jks file, there's one thing you need to know. Put this .jks file somewhere secure, and don't forget the keystore or alias passwords. (To make my life easier, we like to use the same password for my keystore and aliases.) Android mandates us to use the same .jks file to sign any app updates. This means that if we lose the .jks file or its password, we will not update your Android app. We'll have to establish a whole new entry in Google Play, and existing users will be unable to update.

We'll want to use a single keystore file to sign all of our personal or company's Android apps in most circumstances. Remember how we gave the keytool utility a -alias flag, and how that alias had its password? It turns out that a single keystore may have several aliases, and we should establish one for each Android app we develop. (Note: Adding an alias to an existing keystore is simplest in Android Studio.)

So, now that we have this .jks file and have it safely stored somewhere, the remainder of the process is fairly simple. Run the tns build android command, passing it the information we needed to make the .jks file. For example, here's the command we use to generate a Pokémon Types release build.

- tns build android --release

- --key-store-path ~/path/to/tj-vantoll.jks

- --key-store-password my-very-secure-password

- --key-store-alias PokemonTypes

- --key-store-alias-password my-very-secure-password

When the command is finished, we'll have a release .apk file in our program's platforms/android/app/build/outputs/apk folder. Make a note of location of that file since we'll need it in the following step, which is to publish our app on Google Play.

Step 6: Google Play

Google Play is where Android users can locate and install apps, while the Google Play Developer Console allows developers to register and publish apps for consumers to discover.

We will not replicate all of Android's guidance on uploading applications and setting up our store listing here because it's relatively friendly. Instead, we'll share a few pointers that we might find useful when submitting our NativeScript apps to Google Play.

Screenshots

You must offer at least two screenshots of your app in operation on the "Store Listing" tab in the Google Play Developer Console. Although there are other methods for creating these screenshots, I thought we'd outline our favorite method.

Using the tns run android command, we may launch your program in an Android Virtual Device (AVD). The AVDs offer a built-in method for taking screenshots, which can be accessed via the small camera icon in the emulator's sidebar.

The button for taking screenshots from an Android Virtual Device.

Use this button to snap a few screenshots of our app's most essential screens, and the image files will display on our desktop. We could then submit those files directly into the Google Play Developer Console. Still, we prefer to use a service like DaVinci to add a little flare to our screenshots and convert them into a short mini instructional of what our app does. Here are the screenshots we use for Pokémon Types, for example.

Little details like polished screenshots might be the difference between a user clicking the Install button or leaving; therefore, it's well worth investing a few extra minutes in creating high-quality screenshot files.

Feature Graphic

We must also upload a 1024 × 500 "Feature Graphic" image file to Google Play. This file will be shown at the very top of our store listing.

The position of a "Feature Graphic" in a Google Play app listing

Designing a feature graphic may be difficult, and we don't believe we did an excellent job with Pokémon Types as someone who lacks design skills. If we're having problems creating one of these graphics, we may try just utilizing our app's logo against a solid backdrop color. Several major apps, including Facebook, use this strategy.

For its Feature Graphic, many popular programs, such as Facebook, employ a primary symbol.

APK

The .apk file produced in the previous stage of this section should be uploaded to the Google Play Developer Console's "App Releases" section. As a reminder, that file is placed in our program's platforms/android/app/ build/outputs/apk folder. Once we've uploaded our APK and filled out all of our app's details in the Developer Console, we're ready to submit our app. Android app evaluations typically take a few hours, and unless Google notices any issues, our app should be published in Google Play within a half-day or so.

With Android out of the way, we're now prepared to handle iOS.

Step 7: Create an iOS Release Build

There's no point in lying to us; submitting an iOS app to the iOS App Store is one of the most challenging tasks we'll face in our software development career. So, if we get stuck or puzzled throughout these phases, remember that we're not alone; everyone gets annoyed while publishing iOS apps for the first time.

As with the previous stages, we will not go through every step for generating an iOS release build in this section because the required steps vary regularly and because the NativeScript documentation already goes into great length on the subject. What we'll do is lay out a few things that we should be aware of.

Apple Developer Account

We must have an active Apple Developer account to publish iOS apps to the iOS App Store. The program costs $99 USD per year, and we can join up at developer .apple.com/register.

Certificates, Identifiers, and Profiles

Once we have an Apple Developer account, we must use the Apple Developer portal to establish a production certificate, an app ID, and a distribution provisioning profile. This is the most time-consuming aspect of the procedure since it takes some time to learn what each of these different files does and how to utilize them.

The NativeScript documentation includes instructions that will lead us through the process, but the best thing you can do is locate someone who has already gone through these procedures to walk through the essential stages. If we get stuck, post a question on the NativeScript community forum.

Generating Your .ipa File

An .ipa file is the iOS counterpart of an .apk file, and we'll need it to post our program to the iOS App Store.

There are several ways to produce this file with NativeScript. The NativeScript CLI's tns build iOS command with the following option is my favorite method.

- tns build ios --release --for-device

Note: The above command needs us to provide the code signing information in our app/App Resources/iOS/build.xcconfig file specifically, uncomment the CODE SIGN IDENTITY and DEVELOPMENT TEAM lines and provide the proper values. The CODE SIGN IDENTITY should be the same as the name of our distribution iOS certificate, and our DEVELOPMENT TEAM id may be found at https://developer.apple.com/account/#/membership (search for "Team ID").

After this command completes, we will have the .ipa file required in our platforms/ios/build/device folder. Make a note of the file's location since we'll need it in the final stage of this instruction.

Hopefully, we've made it to this point unscathed. We're now ready for the next step, which we wish we could say is simple iTunes Connect.

Step 8: Connect to iTunes

iTunes Connect is essentially Apple's version of the Google Play Developer site, except worse. And by worse, we just mean that it takes at least 50% longer to fill in the required information and figure out what you're supposed to accomplish.

As with the previous stages, I'm not going to walk us through the process of submitting our apps to iTunes Connect. Apple updates the portal far too frequently, and their documentation on iTunes Connect is quite outstanding. However, we will provide some pointers on how to register our software for iOS distribution.

Create a New App

The first step is to register our application. To do so, go to https://itunesconnect.apple.com/, pick "My Apps," then click the "+" button (now in the top-left corner of the page), and then choose "New App."

Use the "New App" link above to register a new app in iTunes Connect.

We'll need to provide some information about our app here, including its name and app id. Here's what we had to say about Pokémon Types.

An example of the information required to register a new app in iTunes Connect.

After giving this information, we will be sent to our app's dashboard, where we will be required to supply further metadata about your application. The majority of this information is rather easy, such as descriptions, price, and so on, but there are a few "interesting" bits to deal with, such as screenshots.

Screenshots

In order to publish our apps, iOS, like Android, requires us to supply screenshot files. Previous versions of iTunes Connect demanded five screenshots for each supported iPhone and iPad resolution, which is as terrible as it sounds.

We just need to upload two sets of screenshots to iTunes Connect now: one for the most significant iPhone devices (5.5-inch displays) and another for the largest iPad devices (12.9-inch devices). Apple still allows us to offer optimal screenshots for every iOS device dimension; however, if we only supply 5.5-inch and 12.9-inch pictures, Apple will automatically rescale our given screenshots for lower display devices.

We could run our program on actual iPhone Plus and iPad Pro devices to capture those screenshots, but we find it significantly easier to get these screenshots through iOS simulators. To do so, launch any iOS simulator and execute our iOS app.

```
tns run ios -emulator
```

Once our iOS simulator is up and running, go to the simulator's "Hardware" -> "Device" menu and select an "iPhone 7 Plus," which is a device that can take 5.5-inch screenshots.

To switch between iOS devices, utilize the Hardware menu in the iOS simulator.

Note: Once we've launched the correct-sized simulator, we must re-run tns run ios-emulator to deploy our app to the new simulator.

When the relevant emulated device is running, we may use the simulator's Cmd + S keyboard shortcut to capture a screenshot of our program, saving the appropriate picture file to our desktop. Take a few screenshots of the most critical areas of our app in operation, much like we did with Android.

When we're finished, utilize the simulator's "Hardware" -> "Device" option to switch to an "iPad Pro (12.9 inches)," as it's a device that can take screenshots of that size. Use the tns run ios-emulator command to deploy our app to the iPad simulator, and then use the Cmd + S keyboard shortcut to retrieve a few iPad-sized photos.

We're all set at this moment. We may use a service like DaVinci to polish our picture files, but when we're finished, drag them into the "App Preview and Screenshots" section of iTunes Connect.

TIP: In this part of iTunes Connect, we may want to consider including an app preview video for our application. App previews are short movies that demonstrate our app in action and may help boost download if done correctly. Refer to Apple's documentation on App preview videos to learn more about them and make successful ones.

Uploading Your .ipa File

We're nearly there! Once we've submitted our information into iTunes Connect, the final step is to correlate our built .ipa file with everything we just typed out. We must specifically complete this step within iTunes Connect.

The default appearance of the "Build" section in iTunes Connect.

According to Apple's reply, there are other ways to upload our .ipa file, including using Xcode or a tool called Application Loader. However, we prefer to use the NativeScript CLI's built-in upload behavior.

To submit our software to iTunes Connect, use the following command:

```
tns publish ios --ipa <path to your ipa file>
```

TIP: Remember to put our.ipa file in the platforms/ios/build/device folder of your app. The complete command I used for Pokeémon Types was tns publish ios – ipa platforms/ios/build/device/pokemontypes.ipa.

And that should be the end of it. However, there is a significant wait between the moment we submit our iOS app and the time it appears in iTunes Connect for some inexplicable reason. We've witnessed delays of as little as 30 seconds and as much as an hour. It's strange, as iTunes Connect offers no indication that anything is going on. So be patient and keep hitting the refresh button until our build file arrives.

The "Build" area in iTunes Connect after uploading a valid.ipa file.

We may be ready to go once we've chosen a build. Hit the vast "Submit for Review" button… and cross fingers.

Apple's assessment of the iOS apps that submit is notoriously irregular. At time of writing, the average review time on the iOS App Store is about two days. It took nearly precisely two days for me to receive a response about Pokémon Types.

TIP: The website appreviewtimes.com/collects app review times to estimate current app review times.

IN NativeScript, WORK WITH DATA

As a developer, we'll be learning the ins and outs of a new framework regularly. Although they differ, most frameworks appear to provide three key user interface (UI)-related functionalities: defining the UI, collecting data, and marrying the two together. NativeScript is no exception: we build our UI with XML, we retrieve data by writing JavaScript code, and NativeScript's data binding framework and observable objects make them work together.

Why Do We Require Dynamic User Interfaces?

We've known the value of dynamic UIs since the inception of the Internet: without them, we'd have to rely on vast volumes of text-based data on web pages. We'd manually update the data whenever it needed to be changed. We were lucky if we just had one copy of the data, but we had many copies in most situations. One option was to store the data centrally and program the UI to pull data from the central location, dynamically modifying what the UI presented.

NativeScript in action walks us through the transition from static to dynamic UIs. We learn to develop static UIs in the book by building the Tekmo app, a mobile storefront for the Tekmo firm, which sells antique video games to aficionados.

Examine the Tekmo app's products page. Although it's difficult to notice, the UI is static and hard-coded.

The Tekmo app's products page, displaying many hard-coded goods.

Each product is hard-coded in the XML file for the product page. Yes, there are few goods, but what if there were dozens? What if the products were to change regularly? Updating hard-coded UI components would rapidly become cumbersome. In addition, we'd have to redeploy the software for consumers to receive an updated version.

Let's try something different: what if we got the Tekmo app's product lists via a file, database, or publicly accessible API endpoint? After obtaining the data, we could update the product listing with it. We'd be able to write less code, and our software would be more dynamic because we wouldn't be hard-coding everything. So, how can we write less code while still allowing customers to create several scrapbook pages? It may not be evident, but we'll use templates to do this.

"Templates allow us to construct the UI element structure of a page without adding the actual text or picture data. When a template is built, the UI components in it serve as placeholders for the actual element displayed on the screen."

The Path to a More Dynamic UI

Let's move from the Tekmo app and look at a second app we created in NativeScript in Action: the Pet Scrapbook. The Pet Scrapbook allows users to create a virtual scrapbook of pages filled with photographs and text to preserve the exciting times in their pet's life.

It makes it logical to design a template in the Pet Scrapbook that represents the structure of a single scrapbook page structure. The template will have placeholders for a pet's name, age, page title, photos, and captions. We may be wondering how this will help us save time and write less code. Consider this in the context of a simple scrapbook.

Assume we're making an actual scrapbook and want to add a page to it. We begin by arranging the page by measuring and using a ruler to verify objects are aligned, straight, and organized similarly to previous pages in our scrapbook. This is done for each image, sticker, and text added to the page. This seems time-consuming, but what if we started with a template:

a page with placeholders for the page's title, our pet's name, images, and other design elements? Adding a new page suddenly becomes a lot easier because the heavy work has been done, and we only need to worry about the page's content.

Using templates in our software is similar to using a scrapbook template. When creating a new page in the NativeScript pet scrapbook, we may use the same design but display different details. We'll reuse the code we wrote for the page because we're utilizing the same template.

Using such a template for the left list view makes sense since we can reuse the template when pages are added, filling in the slots for the pet's image and name. The right-side details view is likewise a good candidate for a template. As the pages on the left are picked, a template might be used to fill in the pet's name, birth date, and so on.

Data Binding

Now that we're familiar with templates, we'd like to show how a single UI template may be reused to display multiple details. The underlying technology utilized to accomplish this is known as data-binding.

"The technique of attaching UI components to objects in code is known as data binding. When a UI element connected to an object in code is changed, the change is reflected in the object or property. Data-bound UI components are those that are related to objects in code."

Data binding refers to the process of connecting a JavaScript object and UI components. Data binding is significant since it eliminates the need to hardcode products into the Tekmo app's product page or update an age field on the Pet Scrapbook app depending on a user's birthday. Before we get started with data binding, let's look at another idea that powers the inner workings of data binding: observables.

"Observables are JavaScript objects that provide alerts to our code when one of their values changes."

We prefer to see observables as students in a classroom: if anything changes, they raise their hands to alert their teacher. It might be because they have a runny nose, need to use the restroom, or want to show their instructor the great robot image they made. It doesn't matter what has changed, but they will raise their hand anytime something has changed to ensure that their instructor knows it. Children are similar to observable objects (also known as observables), except that observables do not raise their hands; instead, they raise an event. We may have observable tracking of our pet's name and birthdate in the context of the Pet Scrapbook.

When one of our app's internal values changes, it may reply to an observable object.

We may be asking how this all fits together at this point. Templates, data binding, observables, and events, these notions, when combined, create the framework upon which we will strive to address the hard-coding challenge.

Data binding, templates, observables, and observable change events are all interconnected.

Data binding is the act of connecting a UI template and an observable. Once connected, the template monitors the observable for change events. When the value of observable changes, an event is triggered. The registered event listener then displays the observable's new value in response to the observable's change.

GETTING OUR APP READY FOR DISTRIBUTION

Before we release our program, configure the information property list and add icons.

Overview

Before we publish a build to App Store Connect or export a build to distribute it outside of the App Store, prepare our Xcode project for distribution. Provide all necessary app information, such as a unique bundle ID, build string, app icon, and launch screen. Choose our options wisely because most of the data is no longer changeable after deploying a build via TestFlight or the App Store.

Set the Bundle ID

When we use a template to create an Xcode project, the bundle ID (CFBundleIdentifier), which uniquely identifies our app throughout the system, defaults to the organization ID appended to the app name you enter in reverse-DNS format; for example, the bundle ID becomes com. example.mycompany.HelloWorld.

Our default bundle ID should be unique if our organization ID is unique across all developers and our app name is unique inside our company. For example, to guarantee that the bundle ID is unique, use our business's domain name as the organization ID.

To deploy our app through TestFlight and the App Store, create an app record in App Store Connect and input the bundle ID from our project. We can't modify the bundle ID once we submit our first build to App Store

Connect, so pick the organization ID carefully when creating the project or adjust the bundle ID later. We can change the name of the app until it is submitted to App Review.

Set the bundle ID for an app target in the Identity section of the project editor's General tab.

Configure the Bundle ID for a Mac App Created with Mac Catalyst

By default, a Mac app produced with Mac Catalyst utilizes the same bundle ID as an iPad app, allowing us to sell the applications together on the App Store as a universal buy.

If we want to offer the Mac version separately, modify the bundle ID in Xcode, then create a new app record in App Store Connect for the Mac app. Select the iOS target in the project editor and then select the Signing and Capabilities pane. Unselect the Use iOS Bundle Identifier option in macOS. Enter a bundle ID for the Mac version in the text field that displays below.

If we have Via-App Purchases or Subscriptions, we must rebuild them in App Store Connect for the Mac app.

Note: If we construct our Mac app using Mac Catalyst using an earlier version of Xcode than 11.4, the Mac app bundle ID will have a maccatalyst prefix followed by the iPad app bundle ID. Change the Derive Mac Catalyst Product Bundle Identifier build parameter from YES to NO to utilize the same bundle ID for both versions.

Configure the Version Number and Build String

The version number (CFBundleShortVersionString) and build string (CFBundleVersion) are used across the system to identify the build of our app uniquely. The report service creates crash, energy, and metrics reports for each build of an app version for apps deployed through TestFlight or the App Store. The version is also displayed in the App Store, and for macOS products, the version number and build string are displayed in the About window.

The build string and version number are supposed to be in the format "[Major].[Minor]. [Patch]," where Patch refers to a maintenance release, such as 10.14.1. The App Store requires both keys.

After we've created the project, enter the version number and build string. Before you archive a build that we intend to share, increment the build string. Then, whenever we build a new version of our app, for example, through App Store Connect, increment the version number.

Before distributing a new build of a macOS program, the build string must be incremented.

Set the version number and build string beneath the bundle ID in the project editor's General pane.

Configure the App Category

On the Software Store, categories help consumers find our app. In Program Store Connect, we specify the primary and secondary categories our app will be displayed on the App Store. For macOS apps, we must also provide the primary category in the project, matching the primary category specified in App Store Connect.

Select a category from the App Category pop-up menu in the Identity section of the project editor's General pane.

Assign a Team to the Project

Assign the project to a team if we haven't previously. For example, if we wish to deploy our software via TestFlight or the App Store, assign all of the targets in a project to an Apple Developer Program team. Xcode produces the appropriate signing assets in the associated developer account when we upload or export our build.

Select a team from the Team pop-up option in the project editor's Signing and Capabilities pane.

Edit the Deployment Info Settings

Edit deployment info settings because some parameters, such as the operating system and devices supported by our program, are later utilized by the App Store.

Choose the oldest operating-system version that can execute our program from the Target pop-up menu in the Deployment Info settings on the project editor's General pane.

Select the compatible devices under the Device column for iOS and watchOS apps. Check both the iPad and Mac boxes under Device to develop a Mac version of an iPad app.

Select the "Supports multiple windows" checkbox at the bottom of the Deployment Info settings to allow multiple windows for an iPad app. Then click the Configure arrow to adjust other options.

Add an App Icon and an App Store Icon

Add an icon to represent our app in different places on a device and in the App Store.

If we wish to release the program through the App Store, include an App Store-specific icon.

The image collection for app icons is already included in a project generated using a template. To view the asset catalogue, click the arrow next to the AppIcon image set in the General pane's App Icons and Launch Images section. Then, drag versions of the app icon to the wells in the asset catalog's detail tab.

The platform determines the position of the App Store icon wells in the asset catalogue. Drag a resolution for the App Store to the App Store iOS well for iOS apps, and drag it to the App Store - 2x well for macOS apps.

Provide a Launch Screen (iOS)

A launch screen is a UI file that appears when our app initially opens and is rapidly replaced by our program's first screen. The start screen simply improves the user experience by giving the user something to look at while launching our program.

When we build a project using a template, we may edit the LaunchScreen.storyboard file. We may also add a start screen file to an existing project.

To Get Access to Protected Resources, Provide Usage Descriptions

When our program attempts to access a protected resource for the first time, the system requests the user for permission. It then produces a window with our app's name and a usage description that you supply. For example, "Our location is utilized to deliver turn-by-turn instructions to our destination" may be the usage description for obtaining the user's location data. When a user provides permission, the system remembers and does not prompt for that resource again. If the user refuses permission, access to that resource and all further attempts are denied.

In the Information Property List, we must include usage descriptions for every protected resource our app accesses, such as the user's location, calendar, reminders, and contacts. Include details of how to use peripherals like the camera and microphone.

Set Up the App Sandbox and Hardened Runtime (macOS)

We must activate Program Sandbox, if we plan to release our macOS app through the App Store. If we want to distribute our macOS program outside the App Store, we must activate hardened runtime and, optionally, App Sandbox.

Configure the Copyright Key (macOS)

Set the copyright key (NSHumanReadableCopyright) in the information property list before uploading our software to App Store Connect for macOS applications.

If we don't explicitly supply a copyright string to the orderFrontStandardAboutPanel(_:) function that displays the About panel in macOS, a translated version of the copyright key is shown instead. If we set the copyright key to @2002-2019 My Company, it will show at the bottom of the About window. For each language that you support, we may localize the information property list.

Add Export Compliance Data

If we distribute our app outside the United States or Canada, it is subject to United States export rules. If our app employs encryption, it must comply with US export regulations. By submitting export compliance information in the Information Property List, we may avoid answering the questions that App Store Connect asks you every time we submit our app for review.

NativeScript SIDEKICK ALLOWS US TO CREATE iOS APPS ON WINDOWS

What Exactly Is a Cloud Build?

When we build an IPA file (for iOS) or an APK file (for Android), we typically use the native SDKs installed on your workstation. The Xcode tools are used for iOS, whereas the Android SDK is used for Android. The issue with developing apps locally is the time it takes to download, install, and set up these tools. Is it feasible? Definitely.

But What If We Weren't Required to Use this Method?

With NativeScript Sidekick, we can practically leave SDK administration to us. Simply instruct Sidekick to develop our app in our cloud, and we will return the IPA and APK app package to us. Your NativeScript materials are sent securely to our cloud servers.

Cloud builds often regarded as significantly slower than local builds. This is understandable given that local builds operate on our hardware, and no data must be sent over a network. Sidekick cloud buildup, on the other hand, is quick. Extremely quick. There's a potential that our cloud builds will be faster than our local builds. Why? Sidekick builds are conducted on the most recent Mac Pros with a high-speed network connection to ensure that our files are uploaded, compiled, and downloaded as quickly as possible.

Is It Still Possible for Us to Build Locally?

If we already have the necessary SDKs installed locally, we can simply select a "local" build inside Sidekick.

As part of our getting started tutorials, we give a complete installation guide for setting up the dependencies necessary for local builds. Sidekick, on the other hand, will install dependencies for us if we lack any.

How Do We Create a Build with Sidekick?

It doesn't get much easier than this. Go to the Run menu in Sidekick when an app is open and select Build.

Choose between iOS and Android builds in the provided window, and make sure Cloud Build is chosen.

"Sidekick caches several intermediate files between builds to guarantee the fastest possible cloud builds. Select Clean build if we need to rebuild our app totally. Please keep in mind that this will drastically slow down the construction."

The catch is that we need a certificate and a provisioning profile to build on iOS. A certificate is also required for publishing to Google Play with Android release builds.

iOS Development on Windows

The ability to build an iOS app from Windows utilizing Sidekick is a significant benefit to Windows developers. However, there are certainly more features that we highlight to make our life easier.

Sidekick also provides the ability to produce certificates for app signing, beginning with a CSR.

Not to add, if we don't already have a valid iOS provisioning profile and certificate pair, Sidekick can produce these for us using a free Apple account.

App store submissions are the final piece of the jigsaw. We can't submit our binary IPA file to the Apple App Store unless we have a Mac. Sidekick, on the other hand, lets us develop and launch directly to the app store.

How Do Continuous Integration Build Work?

As a graphical user interface (GUI) desktop program, Sidekick isn't the first thing that comes to mind when thinking about our continuous integration (CI) process. However, we are actively investigating solutions for exposing our cloud build services through the NativeScript CLI.

PROTECT OUR MOBILE APP

Whether we're creating a classic native app, a cross-compiled app with Appcelerator or Xamarin, a hybrid app with Ionic, or a JavaScript-native app with NativeScript or React Native, app security is a common thread that runs through all of them.

Mobile security is no longer something to be taken casually. Almost everyone has sensitive data, access to company secrets, and protected health information in their pockets.

A Little History:

- Storing user passwords in plain text.

- Sending queries with SSNs in the query string.

- Accepting credit card payments in the absence of SSL.

Users have always depended on public app stores as the ultimate app gatekeepers, functioning as virus guardians and blocking fraudulent API usage. The fact is that we developers must install more security measures before releasing our next fantastic program.

This four-part series on the NativeScript blog will go into various security-related tips and tactics for us to implement in our project. Most of them are quite simple to build because our renowned community of plugin developers has already done the heavy lifting.

- **Part One:** Safeguarding Your Source Code.

- **Part Two:** Data Security at Rest.

- **Part Three:** Ensuring Data Integrity between the Device and the Server.

- **Part Four:** Authentication and Authorization of Enterprise Users.

Source Code Protection

The majority of us have a background in web development. We're used to send our code to a user's browser via a server. Yes, there are intellectual property (code copying) concerns, but we can do nothing to prevent them.

On the other hand, desktop and mobile developers are more accustomed to compiling code into mostly unreadable bits to secure code and reduce attempts to find flaws.

So, how do these challenges be addressed in this new wave of "JavaScript native" apps developed with technologies like React Native and NativeScript? What about hybrid apps created with Ionic?

We hate to break the collective bubble, but source code supplied to the client is fundamentally insecure because it is theoretically readable by the end-user in some way. None of NativeScript, React Native, or Cordova/ Ionic is compiled to native byte code. JavaScript is interpreted on the device in the same way that a web browser does.

So we're a typical native app developer who believes we're safe? Think again – there are a plethora of tools available to decompile our code and read our secrets.

But everything is not lost. Take a look at some methods for encrypting our source code and keeping prying eyes away from our items – preserving our intellectual property while also minimizing any assaults on our applications and backend systems.

Obfuscation and Minification

The first and, admittedly, weakest technique of safeguarding our code is by minification/obfuscation. This is a time-honored method for rendering our code unreadable to human eyes. Uglify, a popular obfuscation package, can accept readable JavaScript code like this.

```
cons app = require("tns-core-modules/application");
cons HomeViewModel = require("./home-view-model");
function onNavigatingTo(args)
  {
    cons page = args.object;
    page.bindingContext = new HomeViewModel();
}
function onDrawerButtonTap(args)
{
    cons sideDrawer = app.getRootView();
    sideDrawer.showDrawer();
}
exports.onNavigatingTo = onNavigatingTo;
exports.onDrawerButtonTap = onDrawerButtonTap;
```

and convert it to significantly less understandable code, like follows:

```
const app=require("tns-core-modules/application");
HomeViewModel=require("./home-view-model");
function onNavigatingTo(o)
{
o.object.bindingContext=new HomeViewModel
}
functiononDrawerButtonTap(o)
{
app.getRootView().showDrawer()
}
exports.onNavigatingTo=onNavigatingTo;
exports.onDrawerButtonTap=onDrawerButtonTap;
```

The NativeScript CLI lets us uglify our app right out of the box, provided we're already using Webpack. To compile and uglify our code, simply run the following command:

```
tns build android|ios --bundle --env.uglify
```

Warning: This is the equivalent of the low-cost bike locks we used in middle school.

It will keep the casual hacker at bay, but the problem is that there are lots of "beautification" resources available that will take uglified code and make it a bit more legible. Using one of these services on the above-mentioned obfuscated code yielded the following results:

```
cons app = require("tns-core-modules/application"),
    HomeViewModel = require("./home-view-model");
function onNavigatingTo(o)
{
    o.object.bindingContext = new HomeViewModel
}
function onDrawerButtonTap(o)
{
    app.getRootView().showDrawer()
}
exports.onNavigatingTo = onNavigatingTo;
exports.onDrawerButtonTap = onDrawerButtonTap;
```

Jscrambler (Protection+++)

We have been in contact with the guys at Jscrambler for many years now, dating back to our days of hybrid app development. Jscrambler is a service that offers extensive JavaScript obfuscation and protection, to the point that the code is unintelligible even after beautifying.

Jscrambler protects our code against tampering by converting our JavaScript into a resistant form to reverse-engineering using automated static analysis techniques. Jscrambler also supports "code locks," limiting when, where, and by whom the JavaScript may be run.

For example, in a NativeScript app, we can execute some JavaScript using Jscrambler.

With NativeScript compatibility confirmed, Jscrambler is undoubtedly worth a try.

We've taken some suitable precautions to safeguard and protect the code we're distributing to our end users at this time.

Restriction of Access via Private App Stores

There are almost no limits on who may download your program from public app stores. Regardless of the aim or audience, a 14-year old in Australia has roughly the same access as an 80-year old in Arizona. Granted, we may limit our applications by age and geo-restrict them to only be available in particular areas, but this has little to do with app security.

A private app store may be a preferable alternative if we build an app that only has to be provided to a single entity (i.e., a group of users or a single company/organization).

Options for Enterprise MAM/MDM

If we work for a large enough firm, chances are we rely on Mobile App Management (MAM) or Mobile Device Management (MDM) software to help protect our internal applications and devices. With a MAM provider, such as MobileIron or AirWatch, we have an internal "business" app store, so we don't have to worry about an unauthorized third party downloading our apps.

Apple Developer Enterprise Program

The Apple Developer Enterprise Program allows us to bypass the public iOS App Store and offer our apps directly to the users of our enterprise. While the cost is more than a standard developer agreement, the distribution flexibility is invaluable.

The code signing and provisioning profile creation processes are identical to the normal technique. Simply put, an extra, distinct provisioning option for in-house/ad hoc app deployment is available.

Android Private Distribution: When it comes to releasing applications outside of Google Play, Google is significantly less conservative. We may build up our private app marketplace (or even design our app that operates as an app store) without troubling the apple cart. Google even lets us distribute programs using email, our website, or a controlled Google Play store.

The only catch is that our end customers must consent to the installation of unfamiliar apps.

If we don't want to build our own, various businesses provide comparable functionality. An example of such a service is Applivery.

Maintain Business Logic on the Cloud

Why not transfer private business logic to a backend system instead of trying to protect it on the device? We can retain complicated business logic on the backend of our mobile app in the same manner that web apps do.

For many cases, whether for security or speed, we may be considerably better off migrating critical business logic from our app to the cloud.

FlexServices, lightweight Node.js microservices supplied by Progress Kinvey, provide a simple method to accomplish this using NativeScript.

We may have certain private business logic in our app that would be better served in the cloud (whether for IP protection, performance reasons, or even hiding other API keys on the server). Instead of retaining this logic in our app, we can use Kinvey to create a FlexService.

For example, the FlexService below collects financial transaction data and rates our performance using a proprietary algorithm:

```
const sdk = require('kinvey-flex-sdk');
function getTransactions(modules)
 {
   return new Promise((resolve, reject) => {
     const store = modules.dataStore({ useUserContext:
false });
     const collection = store.
collection('Transactions');
     const query = new modules.Query();

     collection.find(query, (err, result) => {
       if (err)
```

```
{
        reject(err);
    }

else

{
        resolve(result);
    }
  });
});
}
function determineScore(transactions)
{
  var score = 110;
  transactions.forEach((transaction) => {
    if (transaction.amount < 0)
{
      score -= 5;
    }
    if (transaction.amount > 5)
{
      score += 11;
    }
    if (transaction.category === "restaurant")
{
      score -= 6;
    }
  });
  return score.toString();
}

sdk.service((err, flex) => {
  function getBudgetScore(context, complete, modules)
{
    getTransactions(modules).then((transactions) => {
      complete().setBody({
        score: determineScore(transactions)
      }).done();
    }).catch((err) => {
      complete().setBody(new Error(err)).runtimeError()
.done();
```

```
    });
  }
  flex.functions.register('getBudgetScore',
getBudgetScore);
});
```

And this FlexService is accessed within our app using a Kinvey endpoint:

```
return this.http.post(
    "https://baas.kinvey.com/rpc/kid_<ID>/custom/
BudgetScore",
    {},
    {
        headers: new HttpHeaders({
            "Content-Type": "application/json",
            "Authorization": "Basic <OUR AUTH KEY>"
        })
    }
);
```

Using this strategy, our intellectual property is protected, our business logic is not accessible to our users in any manner and we benefit from the performance and dependability of a fully scaled Kinvey instance.

Take Caution When Sharing Keys

Okay, this may seem overly simple, but it happens far more frequently than we think: make sure we aren't exchanging private keys.

When we utilize GitHub public repositories, we frequently do not control which files are posted. And some bots constantly check repositories for private AWS or Firebase keys, which they then utilize for nefarious purposes, such as:

The simplest approach to avoid this is using a .gitignore file that excludes the.ts/.js file(s) stored in our private keys. Here is the standard .gitignore file we use for our NativeScript projects (assuming TypeScript is used, this also excludes JavaScript files from app directory):

- .vscode/

- .cloud/

- platforms/

- node_modules

- app/**/*.js

- app/**/*.map

- npm-debug.log

- app/keys.*

- hooks/

- app/**/google-services.json

- app/**/GoogleService-Info.plist

This excludes private keys and stops the platforms and node modules folders from being shared (which are entirely unneeded if we're cloning the app, much alone complete of hundreds of files).

In this chapter, we discussed refining apps working with data in NativeScript, as well as releasing an app and preparing an iOS app for release. We also learned about iOS security.

CHAPTER 4

Angular and NativeScript

IN THIS CHAPTER

➤ Creating a NativeScript app with Angular

➤ Using Angular components and routing

➤ Branstein/The NativeScript Book

➤ Angular data binding and services

➤ Using plugins

We discussed working with data in NativeScript and launching an app in the last chapter. We also learned about iOS distribution and security. This chapter will teach us about Angular in NativeScript, including its development, components, Angular data binding, and services.

CREATE A WEB AND MOBILE APPLICATION WITH Angular AND NativeScript

Angular has been available for a few years and has proved effective in creating various types of apps, including online and mobile. The issue, at least, has always been that the experience of developing these various apps has been uneven and frequently perplexing, even though the driving technology has always been the same.

Custom schematics may now be used with the official Angular CLI, which has improved things. So, what does this imply for us? We can take an Angular CLI project, add a NativeScript schematic, and end up with a CLI that works on both web and mobile.

DOI: 10.1201/9781003299394-4

Install the Global NPM Dependencies That Are Necessary

Before we can construct and manage NativeScript apps using the Angular CLI, we must first ensure that we have the necessary global NPM dependencies on our machine. Assuming you already have Node.js installed and configured, run the following command from the command line:

```
npm install -g @angular/cli@6.1.0-beta.0
npm install -g @nativescript/schematics
npm install -g nativescript
```

The Angular CLI, NativeScript CLI, and NativeScript schematics for the Angular CLI will be installed via the instructions listed above. We must keep in mind that schematics are just for building and sustaining projects. For creating and deploying mobile applications, the NativeScript CLI is still necessary.

Take note of the Angular CLI version that is being utilized. As of June 29th, 2018, beta.2 and rc.0 contain several flaws that will be resolved in rc.1. Until then, make sure we're running beta.0.

We won't go into it in this section, but if we want to build locally, our machine must also be set up for Android and iOS development.

Create a New Angular CLI Project That Includes NativeScript Support

We may add NativeScript support to an Angular CLI project after installing the necessary components. While we may apply it to an existing project, we'll start with a new one for simplicity's sake. Execute the following commands from the command line:

```
ng new angular-project
```

The preceding command will generate a new Angular project, which will by default be for web apps rather than native mobile applications. We may add mobile application support by using the following command:

```
ng add @nativescript/schematics
```

Before running the command above, make sure we've gone inside our project. We must be in an Angular CLI-generated project; thus we don't believe schematics can be included in a NativeScript project made using the NativeScript CLI.

If we're genuinely starting from scratch with a code-sharing project, as an alternative we may build an Angular with NativeScript project using the command:

```
ng new --c=@nativescript/schematics --name=angular-
project --shared
```

If we're adding schematics to an existing project, however, the previous command should be used.

Understanding the Schematic Changes and Angular Development Process

When we add the NativeScript schematics to our Angular project, we'll see that it generates a slew of new files and even modifies a few settings files. Don't be concerned about anything negative occurring to our initial idea.

The first thing we'll notice is that we have some .tns.ts and .tns.html files. At first sight, we may believe that we must now handle two separate code-sets, which are not exactly correct.

Because NativeScript is a native mobile application framework, we cannot utilize normal HTML markup for the user interface (UI). As a result, we must maintain both a web UI and a NativeScript UI. We could have a web version and a NativeScript version for everything in TypeScript, but we don't have to. It makes sense in the modules and routing sections because there exist services like NativeScriptRoutingModule and RoutingModule that perform the same thing but are platform specific.

Let's tweak our new app to demonstrate the value of having so many platforms under "nearly" a single CLI. Beginning with the project's src/app/app.routing.tns.ts file, clone it to src/app/app.routing.ts and modify it to look like this:

```
import { NgModule } from '@angular/core';
import { RouterModule } from '@angular/router';
import { Routes } from '@angular/router';
const routes: Routes = [
    { path: '', redirectTo: '/players', pathMatch:
'full' },
];
@NgModule({
    imports: [RouterModule.forRoot(routes)],
    exports: [RouterModule]
})
export class AppRoutingModule { }
```

If we haven't noticed, the differences are in the nomenclature of the modules that are being utilized. We deleted the tns from the filename and used the Angular vanilla modules because this file is for the web.

We're not out of the woods yet. To be more in accordance with the NativeScript version, we must modify our project's src/app/app.module.ts file:

```
import { BrowserModule } from '@angular/
platform-browser';
import { NgModule } from '@angular/core';
import { AppRoutingModule } from './app.routing';
import { AppComponent } from './app.component';
import { BarcelonaModule } from './barcelona/
barcelona.module';
@NgModule({
    declarations: [
        AppComponent,
        AboutComponent
    ],
    imports: [
        BrowserModule,
        AppRoutingModule,
        BarcelonaModule
    ],
    providers: [],
    bootstrap: [AppComponent]
})
export class AppModule { }
```

We'll most likely be playing catch-up with the NativeScript version if we're coming from an existing Angular project. In other words, we're doing the opposite of what we're doing.

The final step is to make any necessary changes to the src/app/app.component.html file. In our Angular project, as of June 2018, we have a default landing page with no routing. We must complete the route configuration. Replace everything in the project's src/app/app.component.html with the following:

```
<router-outlet></router-outlet>
```

We're simply attempting to match the behavior of the two programs. Because the program is new, the NativeScript version achieved far more than the online version. The original material reinforced this.

Our project is complete, but what if we wanted to continue using the Angular CLI? Let's make a new component with the following command:

```
ng g component about
```

The preceding command will utilize the CLI to construct a component called about, resulting in the following:

```
src/app/about/about.component.css
src/app/about/about.component.html
src/app/about/about.component.tns.html
src/app/about/about.component.ts
src/app/about/about.component.spec.ts
```

We mean that we can utilize the Angular CLI in the same way that we would any other Angular application. We'll be left with a .tns. html file to add our custom mobile UI. There are a plethora of additional commands available beyond producing components, so don't feel confined.

Using the NativeScript CLI to Run an Angular CLI Project on Android or iOS

We can now worry about executing our application that the project has been built, modified, and ready to go. In its most basic version, we can verify that the project still functions as a web application. Execute the following commands from the command line:

```
ng serve
```

When the command is finished, go to http://localhost:4200 in our web browser to see it in action. We may also execute the following on a mobile device to launch the application:

```
tns run ios --bundle
```

The command above will launch the app on iOS. We may quickly switch from iOS to Android if that is more convenient for us. The --bundle option is the most significant component of the command. If the program is not packaged, it will crash with a slew of perplexing errors.

Angular 10 Upgrading Suggestions

The NativeScript team has done it again, delivering the most recent Angular 10 support for NativeScript. The recent release of the @nativescript/ schematics package marks another significant step forward in the drive for integrating codebases across online and mobile and improving the developer experience when creating NativeScript with Angular. If we are unfamiliar with @nativescript/schematics, you should look at the package source repository on Github. If we want to give it a try right now, do the following:

```
tns run ios --bundle
npm i -g @angular/cli // You could be needing to
prefix sudo on GNU/Linux and other Unix-like OSes.
npm i -g nativescript // You could be needing to
prefix sudo on GNU/Linux and other Unix-like OSes.
npm i -g @nativescript/schematics // You could be
needing to prefix sudo on GNU/Linux and other Unix-
like OSes.
ng new workspace
cd workspace
ng add @nativescript/schematics
--skipAutoGeneratedComponent

// start apps:
npm run ios
npm run android
ng serve
```

Upgrading Our Angular 10 Project

Updating our project today prepares us for the future NativeScript 7 release because it relies on the current running @nativescript/core rc's, which employ es2017 target builds for Angular 10 compliance. After all, es5 support was formally withdrawn by default. This is a great and welcome update that will be available in NativeScript 7 and will allow for good optimizations with the v8 engine, sophisticated tree shaking, and aligning your NativeScript code with contemporary JS ecosystems.

If we already use NativeScript with Angular and want to keep up to date on project updates, here's how to upgrade to Angular 10:

Warning: Make sure to commit and push our project updates to our remote repository. The procedure includes several modifications that might benefit from a changeset diff against our current project.

Package Should Be Updated .json

package.json is the definitive reference for what our project includes and is dependent on. It presently uses prior versions of our project dependencies for this purpose. Nathan Walker, a TSC member, has described and implemented the form that package.json must take. Based on his suggestion, we wrote a sample node script that reads our existing package.json and, using Spread syntax, changes the packages that need to be updated while keeping our other project dependencies intact. The script also removes the platform version declarations from our package's nativescript section .json, since updating the platform versions alongside the @nativescript/ angular packages is recommended.

1. The file may be downloaded at https://gist.github.com/mahmoudaja wad/351b7e90460b5d78942046049a6f7598. to the root of our project (the same level in which package.json is at).

2. After configuring our working directory to our project path, run: node update_package.tns-ng10.js with our favorite terminal app.

3. The script would be executed, and hopefully, it would result in an Updated package.json!.

   a. If not, and we get the message "package.json.bak" was discovered..., it's likely we tried to execute the script earlier, and our package.json file was already modified.

   b. Open package.json and check to see if the @nativescript/angular package version is set to 10.0.0.

   c. If this is the case, our package.json was most likely previously changed by a previous run of the script.

   d. Otherwise, remove "package.json.bak".

   e. If the problem persists, please let me know to collaborate with us to resolve it.

4. Examine the revised package.json file to ensure that everything is in order.

5. Webpack.config.js should be removed.

   a. Suppose we have made any modifications to webpack.config.js. In that case, we must remember to re-implement them later, as

NativeScript packages will attempt to construct an updated web-pack.config.js file if it is missing.

6. Run npm run clean followed by npm run PLATFORM, where PLATFORM is the platform we seek to deploy the app.

a. The app will not operate because the – no-hmr argument must be supplied when calling tns run PLATFORM. Using npm run PLATFORM will provide us with a shortcut to the required activity.

b. Running projects in preview mode with NativeScript Preview apps for Android and iOS is currently not feasible since an upgrade for Preview applications is required and is in the works: https://github.com/NativeScript/nativescript-schematics/pull/28 6#issuecomment-667577731.

7. If our app doesn't operate, there's a good likelihood that certain imports are broken, which you'll address next. If we prefer to handle things on our own. What you must do is as follows:

a. Package has been updated. Versions of json packages according to this comment.

b. Remove the version of the platform from the nativescript section while keeping the id attribute.

c. Webpack.config.js should be removed.

d. Run npm run clean && npm run PLATFORM, where PLATFORM is the platform we seek to deploy the app.

e. If our app doesn't operate, there's a good likelihood that certain imports are broken, which we'll address next.

Fixing Imports

NativeScript with Angular 10 provides a more uniform framework experience. Importing the framework's tools and classes is one element. This will increase your project's future upgrade resistance to framework changes since the core team can make improvements beneath the hood to the arrangement of the framework classes without altering lots of deep import pathways that can vary significantly from project to project. This implies that some of our project's existing import styles will need to be modified.

To do so, utilize our IDE or editor to search for and substitute the following terms:

```
tns-core-modules
```

Warning: Our search results may include package.json, package-lock.json, package.json.bak, and webpack.config.js. We should not try to change these files.

This package provides all of NativeScript's essential tools and classes. We'd need to find any import statements importing from tns-core-modules and replace them with @nativescript/core. If we have an import statement, we may import from a nested module, for example:

```
import { screen } from 'tns-core-modules/platform';
```

To become, we would need to replace the import as top-level:

```
import { screen } from '@nativescript/core'; // and
not @nativescript/core/platform
// give error
```

Because of the switch from tns-core-modules to @nativescript/core, specific class names have changed, such as screen, which is now Screen. We may determine this by using our IDE or editor's auto-complete combination (often, Ctrl+Space, Cmd+Space) to display all classes accessible in the @nativescript/core package and look for a possible new class name.

Other imports are now completely invalid, such as:

```
import * as applicationSettings from 'tns-core-
modules/application-settings';
```

which must be imported as:

```
import { ApplicationSettings } from '@nativescript/
core';
```

While we don't get any results when searching for tns-core-modules or @nativescript/core/in our codebase, we're done with this stage.

This comment suggests top-level import, which was required for projects to be converted to Angular 10. Deep imports appear to damage projects, and merely switching to top-level importing as suggested in the comments cured upgrading concerns.

```
nativescript-angular
```

Warning: Our search results may include package.json, package-lock.json, package.json.bak, and webpack.config.js. We should not try to change these files.

Similarly, any imports to nativescript-angular must be replaced with @nativescript/angular. The same top-level rule applies here, so if we wind up with search results for @nativescript/angular/after updating our imports, we'll need to remove those deep import lines and rebase them for top-level imports. The import statement in app-routing.module.tns.ts, which is generated by @nativescript/schematics, is a popular example.

```
import { NativeScriptRouterModule } from
'nativescript-angular/router';
```

which, if simply changed to:

```
import { NativeScriptRouterModule } from
'@nativescript/angular/router';
```

It will still damage the app; however, we should remove the deep import entirely as follows:

```
import { NativeScriptRouterModule } from
'@nativescript/angular';
```

Some classes, such as DEVICE, which used to be imported for injecting into our Angular classes, are no longer available following the change. We must now use the Device from @nativescript/core without injecting it.

While we don't get any results when searching for the phrases nativescript-angular or @nativescript/angular/in our codebase, we're done with this step.

Additional Suggestions

As previously said, we may use one of the following methods to execute our NativeScript with Angular 10 app:

```
npm run PLATFORM
tns run PLATFORM --no-hmr
```

When using tns, building the app would fail if the --no-hmr parameter was not present.

If we used this fantastic hack to add re-routing to HMR, we must reverse it because it will damage our program. Simply comment out the import "./livesync-navigation.tns"; line in our main.tns.ts file.

Finally, if we receive the following error:

```
com.tns.NativeScriptException: Calling js method
onCreate failed
```

On Android and iOS, this was followed by the following error:

```
java.lang.IllegalArgumentException: Cannot add a null
child view to a ViewGroup
```

Root should be either UIViewController or UIView

Then we're probably suffering the same problem we did, which is having app.component.tns.html look like this:

```
<page-router-outlet></page-router-outlet>
```

Wrapping the page-router-outlet in any layout component, such as GridLayout or StackLayout, also addressed the problem. As a result, our app.component.tns.html should look something like this:

```
<GridLayout>
    <page-router-outlet></page-router-outlet>
</GridLayout>
```

"**Core Team Note:** It is advantageous to surround a page-router-outlet with a GridLayout, and additional information on the benefits of this layout will be published in the future, which is why it is now the default and needed."

USING Angular, CREATE A NativeScript APP

Angular has been there for a few years and has shown to be useful in the development of a broad variety of applications, including web and mobile applications.

Even while driving technology has always been the same, some developers believe that the experience of designing these various apps may be inconsistent and confusing.

It may, however, be utilized with the standard Angular CLI with modified schematics. This enables us to start a project with the Angular CLI, add a schematic, such as NativeScript, and finish with a CLI that works on both web and mobile.

With the NativeScript schematics, we will utilize the Angular CLI to create a web and mobile-compatible application.

- **Step 1: Installing the NPM requirements**

  Before creating and managing the NativeScript application using the Angular CLI, we must ensure that all NPM requirements are installed on our workstation. If Node.js® and npm are not currently installed on our PC, install them. Now, using the command line, do the following to install the Angular CLI:

  ```
  npm install @angular/cli@6.1.0-beta.0
  ```

- **Step 2: Make an Angular CLI project with NativeScript support**

  Remember that angular schematics are only used to create and maintain projects. Building and deploying mobile apps still necessitate the use of the NativeScript CLI.

  Navigate to the angular-native-project project and run the command below to install the NativeScript CLI and the NativeScript schematics.

  ```
  npm install nativescript@rc
  npm install --save-dev @nativescript/schematics
  @rc
  ```

  Now that we've installed all of the required dependencies, we can add NativeScript functionality to our new Angular CLI project. Navigate to the command line and run the following command:

  ```
  ng new angular-native-project
  ```

  The preceding will generate a new Angular project, which will by default be for web apps rather than native mobile applications.

  The schematics cannot be included if we are in a project built using the Angular CLI; for example, if we created a NativeScript project with the NativeScript CLI, the schematics cannot be included.

  ```
  ng add @nativescript/schematics
  ```

Code-Sharing Initiative: We may also easily establish a code-sharing project for us, allowing to build for both web and mobile by using a –shared parameter. As an example:

```
ng new -c=@nativescript/schematics angular-native-
project2 --prefix=my --no-theme --style=scss
--no-webpack
```

- **Step 3: Schematic modifications and the Angular development process**
  After adding the NativeScript schematics to our project, we'll note that some new files with the .tns extension have been produced, and a few configuration files have been modified. Look in the project directory for the .tns.ts and .tns.html files.

  Because NativeScript is a native mobile application framework, we cannot utilize standard HTML markup for the UI. As a result, we will need to maintain both a web UI and a NativeScript UI. When it comes to TypeScript, we can have a web version and a NativeScript version for everything, but we don't have to.

  However, it makes sense in the modules and routing sections because services like NativeScriptRoutingModule and Routing Module perform the same thing but are platform-specific.

```
src/app/app.routing.ts
import {NgModule }from "@angular/core"; import
{RouterMod ule }from "@angular/router"; import
{Routes }from "@angular/router";
const routes: Routes = [
{path: '', redi rectTo: '/players', pathMatch:
'full' },
];
@NgModule({
imports: [RouterModule.forRoot(routes)], exports:
[RouterMod ule]
})
export class AppRoutingModule {}
```

The only distinction here is in the nomenclature of the modules in use. We deleted the tns from the filename and utilized the vanilla Angular modules because this file will be used for the web.

Following that, we must modify the project's src/app/app.module.ts file to be more in line with the NativeScript version:

```
src/app/app.module.ts
import { BrowserModule }from '@angular/platform-bro
wser '; import { NgModule }from '@angular/core';
import { AppRoutingModule }from './app.routing' ;
import { AppComponent }from './app.component ';
@NgModule ({
declarations: [ AppComponent,
],
imports: [
BrowserModule, AppRoutingModule,
],
provide rs :[],
bootstrap: [AppComponent]
})
export class AppModule {}
```

The final step is to make changes to the src/app/app.component.html file. At the time of writing, the Angular project contains a default landing page with no routing. As a result, we must complete the routing configuration. Replace everything in src/app/app.component. html with the following:

```
<router-outlet></router-outlet>
```

We're attempting to match the behavior of the two applications. Because the program is still in its early stages, the NativeScript version did far more than the plain web version. The original material reinforced this.

Our project is complete at this time. But what if we require a new component in the future? Let's give this a try using the following command:

```
ng g component home
```

The command above will utilize the CLI to build a component named home. As a consequence, the following files will be generated:

- src/app/home/home.component.css

- src/app/home/home.component.html

- src/app/home/home.component.tns.html

- src/app/home/home.component.ts

- src/app/home/home.component.spec.ts

We may utilize the Angular CLI in the same way that we would utilize any other Angular application. We'll finish up with a.tns .html file to which we may add your custom mobile UI.

- **Step 4: Using the NativeScript CLI to run an Angular CLI project on Android or iOS**
We can now start the application when the project has been built, modified, and ready. To see if the project still works as a web application, use the following commands:

```
ng serve
```

When the command is finished, navigate to http://localhost:4200 in your web browser to see it in action. To run the program on a mobile device, use the following command:

```
tns run ios --bundle
```

The command above will launch the app on iOS. And, if necessary, we can quickly swap the iOS component to Android. The --bundle flag is the most crucial component of the command. If we don't package the program, it will crash with a slew of issues.

Angular BOOTSTRAP

The Bootstrap Process

A typical NativeScript program begins by initializing global objects, configuring global CSS rules, and building and navigating the main page. Angular is unconcerned about any of this; all it needs is a location in the DOM to attach. Naturally, Angular apps must handle their initialization: modules, components, directives, routes, and DI providers. To make both paradigms operate together in a NativeScript Angular project, we create a wrapper platform object, platformNativeScriptDynamic, which sets up a NativeScript application and may bootstrap the Angular framework in a default place on the main UI page.

```
platformNativeScriptDynamic().bootstrapModule(AppModule);
```

One of our main design goals here is to provide an interface almost identical to the default Angular bootstrap process so that folks who are acquainted with the web version of Angular can get started with as little friction as possible.

NativeScript Application Option

NativeScript application settings are set when the program is launched. Angular apps might be an issue because the normal application startup procedure is buried behind the platformNativeScriptDynamic black box. We added an extra AppOptions parameter to the platform startup method to enable modifications, allowing us to preconfigure some parts of our application's behavior. At present, they are as follows:

- **cssFile:** Overrides the path to a file containing global CSS rules applied to all visual objects in the application. The default path is app.css.

- **createFrameOnBootstrap:** If our application does not utilize a page-router-outlet, we will not receive the default Page and Frame, which means we will not be able to inject them into our components or display the ActionBar. We may use the bootstrap createFrameOnBootstrap boolean option to make things seem as they did before 4.0.0:

```
platformNativeScriptDynamic({ createFrameOnBootstrap:
true });
```

Customizing DI Providers

The dependency injection (DI) mechanism is used to customize several features of Angular applications. NgModules are often the mechanism for configuring DI providers and exposing them to all application objects. Several Angular libraries, such as the router and the http client, have their modules for registering providers. NativeScript wraps the built-in modules (router, forms, and HTTP) that should be utilized in mobile apps:

```
import { platformNativeScriptDynamic,
NativeScriptModule } from "nativescript-angular/
platform";
import { NgModule } from "@angular/core";
import { NativeScriptRouterModule } from
"nativescript-angular/router";
import { NativeScriptHttpModule } from "nativescript-
angular/http";
```

```
import { NativeScriptFormsModule } from "nativescript-
angular/forms";
import { routes } from "./app.routes";
import { AppComponent } from "./app.component";
@NgModule({
    declarations: [
        AppComponent,
    ],
    bootstrap: [AppComponent],
    imports: [
        NativeScriptModule,
        NativeScriptHttpModule,
        NativeScriptRouterModule,
        NativeScriptRouterModule.forRoot(routes),
    ],
})
class AppModule {}
platformNativeScriptDynamic().bootstrapModule(AppModule);
```

Objects Injected by the Platform

Because the DI system is so important in Angular apps, it makes sense to expose specific platform objects to client code. It is thus as easy as defining a constructor parameter of the appropriate type to access them. For example, here's how the component below obtains a native Page object:

```
@Component({
    selector: "user-details",
    template: "..."
})
export class UserDetailsView {
    constructor(private page: Page) {
    }
}
```

Autoinjected Objects

- **"ui/page". Page:** The native page on which the component renders. When loading components on separate pages, the router implementation ensures that the right instance is injected.

- **"platform".Device:** Information about the device on which the program is executing.

Advanced Bootstrap

Certain application circumstances may need bootstrapping an Angular app within an existing NativeScript app. The requirement for this typically emerges in automated tests that require the creation and destruction of apps in various configurations. Advanced bootstraps may also be beneficial for moving vanilla NativeScript apps to Angular-- we may begin the transfer by integrating Angular and building new features with it, then migrate old features one at a time.

The sophisticated bootstrap API entry point is our buddy's platformNativeScriptDynamic factory method, but this time, the bootInExistingPage application option must be passed. We'll also need a DI provider to return the visual element of the application's root view. Here's an example of a normal bootstrap:

```
const root = new StackLayout();
const rootViewProvider = {provide: APP_ROOT_VIEW,
useValue: root};
@NgModule({
    //...
    providers: [
        rootViewProvider,
    ]
})
class AdvancedBootstrapModule {}
platformNativeScriptDynamic({bootInExistingPage: true})
.bootstrapModule(AdvancedBootstrapModule);
```

NAVIGATION

In this piece, we'll go through how to use Angular to navigate in a NativeScript application and present some practical examples of typical mobile navigation patterns.

The Angular Component Router is used for navigating in Angular. We can find thorough instructions on how to operate the router here. In this topic, we will assume that we are familiar with the fundamental ideas and will focus on the intricacies of implementing them in a NativeScript program.

NativeScript Route Module

NativeScript enhances the Angular RouterModule with its NativeScriptRouterModule. It includes several modifications and changes required for routing to operate in a mobile context and choices for bringing the entire native mobile navigation UX to Angular.

There are a few UX details that are difficult to duplicate using the default Angular router alone:

- Transitions in native navigation.

- Handling back navigation – on Android, the hardware back button, and on iOS, the navigation bar back button.

- View state preservation while traveling back in the mobile navigation lifecycle.

- Mobile-specific history – instead of global history, retain history for each navigation controller.

- BottomNavigation, Tabs, SideDrawer, Modal View, and more mobile lateral navigation widgets.

NativeScript adds them to Angular via the extensions, directives, and techniques listed below:

- **page-router-outlet:** An alternative to the conventional router-outlet that acts as a placeholder for where native mobile navigation will take place.

- nsRouterLink is a routerLink directive that works with mobile gestures as an alternative to the standard routerLink directive.

- The RouterExtensions class, like the Router and Location classes, provides a native mobile navigation API.

- **Custom RouteReuseStrategy:** This approach requires Angular to cache and reuse components loaded in a page-router-outlet in line with the native navigation lifecycle.

- **Custom PlatformLocation and LocationStrategy:** Instead of global linear history, this approach preserves history per outlet.

Page-Router-Outlet

The page-router-outlet in NativeScript is analogous to the router-outlet in Angular. It acts as a stand-in for native mobile navigation. Each page-router-outlet generates a NativeScript Frame internally, and each component displayed by the router in the outlet is wrapped in a Page widget. This is the primary integration point for Angular's native navigation. Because of the Frame and Page combo, we may also utilize the ActionBar widget in these components.

We propose utilizing the page-router-outlet for our primary mobile navigation pattern and the standard router-outlet for internal component navigations if necessary. We may alternatively use merely the router-outlet if it makes more sense in our situation.

Router Link

The Angular routerLink directive cannot be used in a NativeScript application. NativeScript has its nsRouterLink directive that works similarly. It also supports two NativeScript-specific properties, which we may add to our nsRouterLink element in the HTML.

- **pageTransition:** We may use this parameter to describe the native transition for nsRouterLink navigation. True, false, one of the standard transitions mentioned above, or a new NavigationTransition object are valid values.

- **clearHistory:** This attribute accepts a boolean value and specifies whether the navigation initiated by the nsRouterLink will clear the current outlet's navigation history.

  ```
  <Button text="Button" [nsRouterLink]="['/main']"
  pageTransition="slide" clearHistory="true"></Button>
  ```

Router Extention

The RouterExtensions class provides methods for imperative navigation, similar to how the Angular Router and Location classes provide navigation. Simply inject the class into our component's constructor to use it:

```
import { RouterExtensions } from "nativescript-
angular/router";
@Component({
    // ...
})
export class MainComponent {
    constructor(private routerExtensions:
RouterExtensions) {
    }
}
```

Here is a list of the available ways:

- **navigate()**: Similar to Angular Router's navigate() function, enables navigations in a page-router-outlet.

- **navigateByUrl()**: Similar to the preceding method, this is an alternative to the Router navigateByUrl() method, which works with page-router-outlet.

- back() is the equivalent of the Angular Location back() function. It will return to the last outlet visited.

- **canGoBack()**: It is a NativeScript-introduced method. It produces a boolean result indicating if the user can return to the previous route.

- **backToPreviousPage()**: This function is identical to back(), except it skips navigations performed in an Angular router-outlet.

- **canGoBackToPreviousPage()**: This function provides a boolean value indicating if the user can travel back to a route that was loaded in a page-router-outlet.

Custom Route Reuse Strategy

NativeScript also imports a custom RouteReuseStrategy, which alters the lifespan of components browsed through a page-router-outlet.

A component in the Angular router-outlet is destroyed when we navigate away from it and recreate when we go back to it. The component lifespan differs in no way between forward and backward navigation.

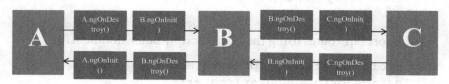

Outlet of Router.

The system will keep the navigation views alive in a native mobile application so that when you return to them, their view state will be preserved. Views are only damaged when we move away from them. Because the page-router-outlet contains native navigations, the lifespan of its components must mirror the lifecycle of the native views. The special NSRouteReuseStrategy does this.

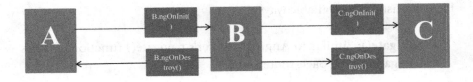

Outlet of Page Router.

When we go ahead to the next page, we may wish to do specific housekeeping steps (e.g., unsubscribe from a service to stop updates). If we're using page-router-outlet, we can't do it in the ngOnDestroy() hook since it won't be invoked when we go ahead. We may conduct the cleaning by injecting the Page instance within our component and attaching it to page navigation events (e.g., navigatedFrom). We may get a list of all available page events here.

Configuration

Typically, router configuration consists of the following steps.

- Make a RouterConfig object that associates pathways with components and parameters:

```
export const routes = [
    { path: "log-in", component: LoginComponent },
    { path: "grocerie", component:
GroceryListComponent },
    { path: "grocery/:id", component:
GroceryComponent }
];
```

- Import our routes using the NativeScriptRouterModule API:

```
import { NativeScriptRouterModule } from
"nativescript-angular/router";

@NgModule({
    bootstrap: [GrocerieApp],
    imports: [
        NativeScriptRouterModule,
        NativeScriptRouterModule.forRoot(routes)
    ]
})
export class GrocerieAppModule { }
```

- To begin our program, as normal, send our module to the bootstrap-Module function:

```
import {platformNativeScriptDynamic} from
"@nativescript/angular";
platformNativeScriptDynamic().bootstrapModule(Groc
erieAppModule);
```

Mobile Navigation Patterns

The act of moving across the screens of your application is referred to as navigation. Based on the information it attempts to display, each mobile app has its distinct navigation schema. The following diagram depicts a typical mobile navigation scenario.

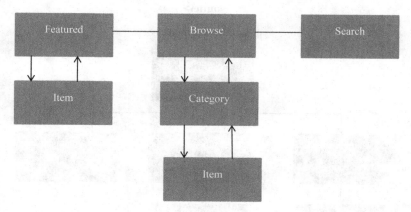

Scenario of Mobile navigation.

According to the schema, there are three main navigational directions a user can go in while using mobile navigation:

- **Forward:** Refers to moving to the next level of the hierarchy and selecting a screen.

- **Backward:** Refers to returning to a screen on a prior level of the hierarchy or chronologically.

- **Lateral:** Navigating between screens on the same level of the hierarchy is referred to as lateral.

In terms of navigation choices, the combination of NativeScript with Angular is quite strong. Angular has its well-known navigation system as well as a router. NativeScript, on the other hand, gives developers access to native mobile navigation patterns. Because of the nature of the integration, we can employ any of them or a mix that best meets our needs. In the following sections, we will show how to implement several mobile navigation patterns.

Angular Navigation

The default Angular navigation is designed for use on the web with a browser. It solely provides methods for forward and backward travel, no lateral navigation. However, the schema above can be implemented by merely moving ahead and backward.

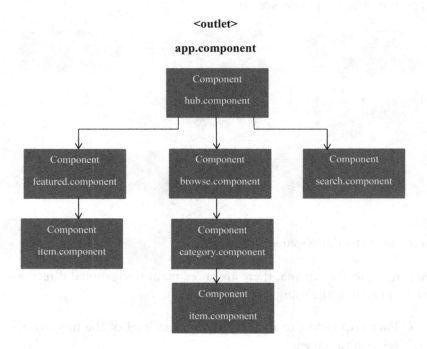

Component of app.

In mobile jargon, this is known as the hub navigation pattern, in which we have a screen that navigates to all of our application's capabilities.

We'll utilize a router-outlet in conjunction with the nsRouterLink directive and the back() function of the Angular Location class. Only two of the components are shown in the code example below. For a more detailed example, see the playground demo below.

APP-ROUTING.MODULE.TS

```
import { NgModule } from "@angular/core";
import { Route } from "@angular/router";
import { NativeScriptRouterModule } from
"nativescript-angular/router";
import { HubComponent } from "./hub.component";
import { FeaturedComponent } from "./featured.
component";
import { ItemComponent } from "./item.component";
import { BrowseComponent } from "./browse.component";
import { CategoryComponent } from "./category.
component";
import { SearchComponent } from "./search.component";
const route: Route = [
    { path: "", redirectTo: "/hub", pathMatch: "full" },
    { path: "hub", component: HubComponent },
    { path: "featured", component: FeaturedComponent },
    { path: "item", component: ItemComponent },
    { path: "browse", component: BrowseComponent },
    { path: "category", component: CategoryComponent },
    { path: "search", component: SearchComponent },
];
@NgModule({
    imports: [NativeScriptRouterModule.forRoot(routes)],
    exports: [NativeScriptRouterModule]
})
export class AppRoutingModule { }
```

Forward Navigation

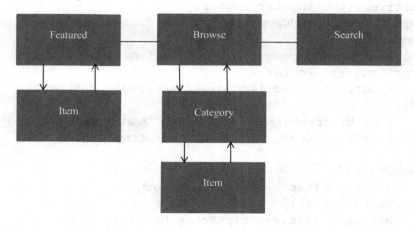

Navigation of forwarding.

Because we are moving down in our navigation hierarchy, forward navigation is also known as downward navigation. A page-router-outlet would handle this form of navigation in a NativeScript Angular app.

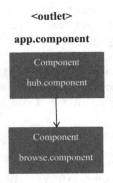

Using a page-router-outlet has the extra benefit of allowing us to use the ActionBar widget in our component. When we browse to a second page on iOS, the widget automatically adds a back button. On Android, the page-router-outlet takes advantage of the hardware back button, which allows us to go back to your components. Check out the playground example, which is located below the code sample.

APP-ROUTING.MODULE.TS

```
import { NgModule } from "@angular/core";
import { Routes } from "@angular/router";
import { NativeScriptRouterModule } from
"nativescript-angular/router";
import { FeaturedComponent } from "./featured.
component";
import { ItemComponent } from "./item.component";
const routes: Routes = [
    { path: "", redirectTo: "/featured", pathMatch:
"full" },
    { path: "featured", component: FeaturedComponent },
    { path: "item", component: ItemComponent }
];
@NgModule({
    imports: [NativeScriptRouterModule
.forRoot(routes)],
    exports: [NativeScriptRouterModule]
```

```
})
export class AppRoutingModule { }
```

Backward Navigation

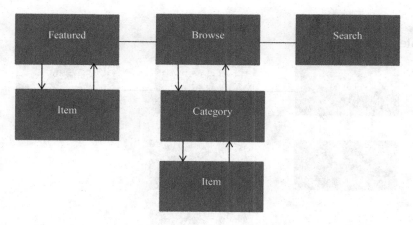

Navigation of Backward.

It is also known as upward navigation since you are moving up in our navigation hierarchy. This style of navigation reflects the inverse of forward navigation. Simply invoke the RouterExtensions back() function to force a navigation back to the prior route. Here's an example of how to accomplish that in the item.component:

ITEM.COMPONENT.TS

```
import { Component, OnInit } from "@angular/core";
import { RouterExtensions } from "nativescript-
angular/router";
@Component({
    selector: "Item",
    templateUrl: "./item.component.html",
    styleUrls: ['./item.component.css']
})
export class ItemComponent implements OnInit {
    constructor(private routerExtensions:
RouterExtensions) {
    }
    ngOnInit(): void {
    }
```

```
goBack(): void {
    this.routerExtensions.back();
}
}
```

Lateral Navigation

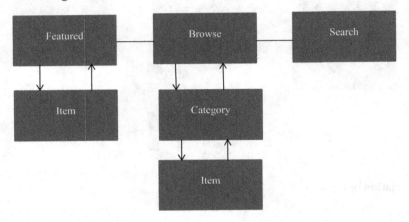

Navigation of Lateral.

Implementing lateral navigation in NativeScript often entails incorporating sister router outlets into our navigation and allowing the user to move between them. This is usually performed by utilizing certain navigation components. BottomNavigation, Tabs, SideDrawer, Modal View, and even the page-router-outlet are examples of these, each of which provides a distinct mobile navigation pattern.

Hub Navigation

The hub navigation pattern is the most straightforward and straightforward approach to execute lateral navigation. It comprises a screen called a hub that has navigation buttons that lead to various functionalities. In essence, this design employs the same principle for the lateral movement that it does for forward travel. We can do this in NativeScript by using a page-router-outlet and having one Component act as the hub screen.

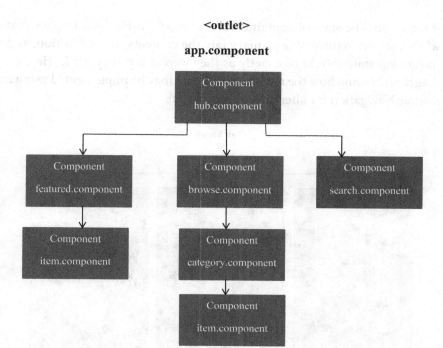

Navigation of Hub.

HUB.COMPONENT.TS

```
import { Component, OnInit } from "@angular/core";
@Component({
    selector: "Hub",
    templateUrl: "./hub.component.html",
    styleUrls: ['./hub.component.css']
})
export class HubComponent implements OnInit {
    constructor() {
    }

    ngOnInit(): void {
    }
}
```

Bottom Navigation and Tab Navigation

The TabView component allows the user to browse freely between many UI containers at the same level. This component's significant feature is that it maintains the state of containers that are not visible. This implies that when the user returns to a primary tab, the contents, scroll position, and navigation state should be exactly as they were when they left it. Here's a diagram showing how the navigation schema may be implemented using a BottomNavigation (or alternatively with Tabs).

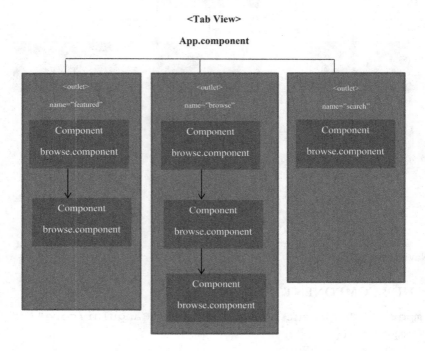

Navigation of Bottom.

The BottomNavigation container handles lateral navigation logic automatically by presenting the user with tabs from which to choose. To create a BottomNavigation, just describe the UI of each container using a TabItemContent and specify the title and icon using the matching tab-StripItem (details on the basic structure here). The TabContentItem component represents each UI container. You may enable forward and backward navigation within each container, just like we do with other containers, by embedding a page-router-outlet in it. In this situation, three sibling outlets are required. Using named outlets with the Angular router is the method to do this.

Using named outlets with the Angular router is the method to do this. Each of our outlets will be called for the functionality it represents.

The BottomNavigation widget also has two essential lateral navigation features:

- The selectedIndex attribute may be used to browse between tabs programmatically.

- The selectedIndexChanged event is used to handle the user's navigation across tabs.

Here's a code sample for the BottomNavigation declaration, which corresponds to the diagram above. See the whole playground example after the code sample.

APP-ROUTING.MODULE.TS

```
import { NgModule } from "@angular/core";
import { Routes } from "@angular/router";
import { NativeScriptRouterModule } from
"nativescript-angular/router";
import { FeaturedComponent } from "./featured.component";
import { ItemComponent } from "./item.component";
import { BrowseComponent } from "./browse.component";
import { CategoryComponent } from "./category.component";
import { SearchComponent } from "./search.component";
const routes: Routes = [
    { path: "", redirectTo: "/(featured:featured//
browse:browse//search:search)", pathMatch: "full" },

    { path: "featured", component: FeaturedComponent,
outlet: "featured" },
    { path: "item", component: ItemComponent, outlet:
"featured" },
    { path: "browse", component: BrowseComponent,
outlet: "browse" },
    { path: "category", component: CategoryComponent,
outlet: "browse" },
    { path: "item", component: ItemComponent, outlet:
"browse" },
    { path: "search", component: SearchComponent,
outlet: "search" },
];
@NgModule({
    imports: [NativeScriptRouterModule.forRoot(routes)],
    exports: [NativeScriptRouterModule]
})
export class AppRoutingModule { }
```

Model View Navigation

A frequent mobile navigation strategy is to open a new navigation controller as a full-screen modal window. Opening the modal window in this scenario symbolizes lateral travel to a new feature. The integrated page-router-outlet may then be used to go forward and backward in this feature. When you close the modal, we will be navigated laterally back to where the modal view was accessed. The following diagram shows how the navigation paradigm may be implemented using modal views.

In NativeScript Angular, you open a modal view by injecting the ModalDialogService into our component and using its showModal() function. There are two arguments to this method: a component and an options object. The component sent to the showModal() function becomes the base of the modal view UI container. We are traveling to this component laterally rather than forwardly, and we are doing it without the router. It does not have a matching route, and we cannot register it as a route in our routes configuration; instead, we must manually register it as an Angular Entry Component in our module.

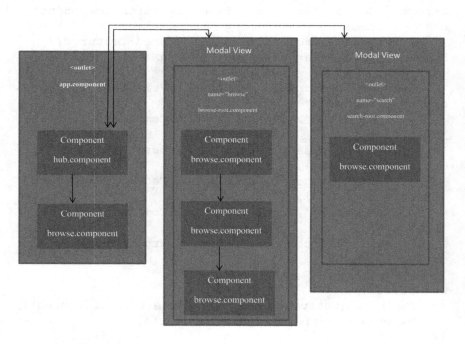

Model View Navigation

When the modal view is opened, the component's UI is rendered. To put the diagram above into action, we must create forward navigation within the modal. We do this by including a page-router-outlet in the component's template and using the component's ngOnInit hook to go to the first route in the modal. We're also giving the outlet a name since we will have two modals, so their outlets will be siblings. In general, we advocate naming router outlets within modal views.

Close a modal view by invoking the closeCallback() function of the injected params or by obtaining a NativeScript View and calling its closeModal() method.

The example shows how to construct the Search modal view and page from the design above. See the whole playground example after the code sample.

APP-ROUTING.MODULE.TS

```
import { NgModule } from "@angular/core";
import { Routes } from "@angular/router";
import { NativeScriptRouterModule } from
"nativescript-angular/router";

import { FeaturedComponent } from "./featured
.component";
import { ItemComponent } from "./item.component";
import { BrowseComponent } from "./browse.component";
import { CategoryComponent } from "./category.
component";
import { SearchComponent } from "./search.component";
const route: Route = [
    { path: "", redirectTo: "/featured", pathMatch:
"full" },
    {
        path: "featured", component:
FeaturedComponent, children: [
            { path: "browse", component:
BrowseComponent, outlet: "browse" },
            { path: "category", component:
CategoryComponent, outlet: "browse" },
            { path: "item", component: ItemComponent,
outlet: "browse" },

            { path: "search", component: SearchComponent,
outlet: "search" },
        ]
```

```
    },
    { path: "item", component: ItemComponent },
];
@NgModule({
    imports: [NativeScriptRouterModule.
forRoot(routes)],
    exports: [NativeScriptRouterModule]
})
export class AppRoutingModule { }
```

SideDrawer Navigation

NativeScript UI's built-in components include the SideDrawer component. It allows the user to open a hidden view, such as a drawer, containing navigation controls or settings from the screen's edges. A SideDrawer may be used to build a variety of navigation patterns. A typical application would be to add UI controls that accomplish one of two things:

- Forward navigation entails moving forward in a page-router-outlet.

- Open a modal view using lateral navigation.

The easiest navigation pattern to create is the hub navigation pattern; however, the SideDrawer serves as the hub this time.

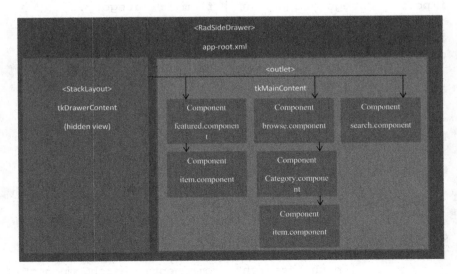

SideDrawer Navigation

The component, unlike the BottomNavigation, does not offer navigation logic automatically. Instead, it is designed with more flexibility in mind and allows you to change its content. It exposes two UI containers with two directives: tkDrawerContent contains the UI of the concealed side view, and tkMainContent includes the UI that will be displayed on the screen. To put the diagram above into action, insert a page-router-outlet into the main content container. Three buttons can be included in the concealed drawer content. They will each navigate to one of the three features. See the whole playground example after the code sample.

APP-ROUTING.MODULE.TS

```
import { NgModule } from "@angular/core";
import { Route } from "@angular/router";
import { NativeScriptRouterModule } from
"nativescript-angular/router";
import { FeaturedComponent } from "./featured
.component";
import { ItemComponent } from "./item.component";
import { BrowseComponent } from "./browse.component";
import { CategoryComponent } from "./category.
component";
import { SearchComponent } from "./search.component";
const route: Route = [
    { path: "", redirectTo: "/featured", pathMatch:
"full" },
    { path: "featured", component: FeaturedComponent
},
    { path: "item", component: ItemComponent },
    { path: "browse", component: BrowseComponent },
    { path: "category", component: CategoryComponent
},
    { path: "search", component: SearchComponent },
];
@NgModule({
    imports: [NativeScriptRouterModule.
forRoot(routes)],
    exports: [NativeScriptRouterModule]
})
export class AppRoutingModule { }
```

DATA BINDING

Data Binding is a fundamental element in both the NativeScript and the Angular frameworks. Data Binding, by definition, refers to a link (binding) between a Data Model (Model) and a UI. Because this link or interaction mainly concerns data, we refer to it as Data Binding.

One-Way vs. Two-Way Data Binding

Data flows can occur in a variety of ways (data bindings):

- **One-way data binding:** It is the most often used method of binding from Model to UI. A text saved in Model and shown on the UI in a text area control is an excellent example of such coupling.

- **One-way to the source (to model):** Binding that changes Model in response to UI action. The best illustration of this is a button click event (tap).

- **Two-way data binding:** Binding that combines the two preceding methods of binding. A common example is a text box field that receives its value from the Model and alters the Model based on user input.

The NativeScript-angular plugin makes it easier to determine which data binding will be utilized. The binding infrastructure's NativeScript component ties Model data to real native components (Android and iOS). The Angular component is used to provide proper binding context, change detection, and notifications. Using data binding in a NativeScript-Angular application is similar to using data binding in a conventional Angular web application.

Let's look at several instances of data binding with the NativeScript-angular plugin.

- One-way data binding entails enclosing the target (UI) property in square brackets.

  ```
  <Label [text]='model.mytext' ></Label>
  ```

- One-way source data binding entails enclosing the source event in brackets.

  ```
  <Button (tap)='onButtonTap($event)'></Button>
  ```

- Two-way data binding entails encircling the target property with square and normal brackets.

```
import { NativeScriptFormsModule } from
"nativescript-angular/forms"
@NgModule({
    imports: [
        NativeScriptModule,
        NativeScriptRouterModule,
        NativeScriptFormsModule, // RIGHT HERE
    ],
})
```

Two-way data binding was the default binding method in Angular 1.x. However, the status of two-way data binding is not the same with Angular, owing to too many performance issues created by the ambiguity of what or who triggered the change of the value within Model, which sometimes leads in far too many changes (and change notifications). So, by default, Angular does not support two-way data binding; instead, it utilizes events to tell the Model that something has changed.

```
<TextField [(ngModel)]='model.mytext'></TextField>
```

When utilizing two-way data binding with Angular, there are several constraints. Instead of the property name, the ngModel directive is used to initiate two-way binding. Under the hood, this produces two basic one-way and one-way to source data bindings:

```
<TextField [(ngModel)]='model.mytext' ></TextField>
<!-- becomes -->
<TextField [ngModel]='model.mytext'
(ngModelChange)='model.mytext=$event' ></TextField>
```

This is how Angular handles two-way data binding. It works in virtually all circumstances, except that we can only utilize one property with two-way data binding (in the case of TextField this is the text property). The ngModel directive also provides an interface for updating properties in both ways properly. The NativeScript-Angular plugin offers the underlying architecture to enable native controls using ngModel directive for all NativeScript controls (the same way as Angular syntax). It is accomplished by defining a single value property for each control that can be utilized with ngModel syntax. The following are the accessible properties:

- TextField, TextView, and SearchBar all have a text attribute.
- DatePicker is a date picker.
- TimePicker is a time-related property.
- ListPicker and SegmentedBar have a property called selectedIndex.
- The switch is checked Property.
- Slider is a Value attribute.

Interpolation

A NativeScript-Angular application may also use the Angular mustache ({{}}) syntax for binding, often known as interpolation. It is simply another type of one-way binding used in the middle of a text.

```
<Label text='{{model.deliveryHour}}:{{model
.deliveryMinute}}'></Label>
```

Data Converters

Data inside a Data Model is frequently stored in a manner optimized for the most outstanding performance of actions such as search, replace, and so on. Unfortunately, the way computers store data differs significantly from that in a human-readable format. The Date object is perhaps the finest example. Date in JavaScript is an extremely large number representing milliseconds from January 1, 1970, which means nothing to a person. Here comes the usage of data converters, which are essentially functions that format the data (from the Model) in a human-readable manner (display in UI).

Angular employs the same notion and refers to it as a pipe (as in UNIX pipe) – a value is supplied to the pipe function, which alters it, and the final result is shown to the user. Using pipe is straightforward and follows the same syntax as UNIX pipe.

```
<Label [text]='model.deliveryDate | date:"fullDate"'
></Label>
```

Pipes, like UNIX pipes, can be chained and used sequentially, with each pipe receiving the result of the preceding pipe or the value of the property:

```
<Label [text]='model.deliveryDate | date:"fullDate" |
testPipe' ></Label>
```

USING PLUGINS

NativeScript plugins are npm packages that have some native functionality added to them. As a result, locating, installing, and deleting NativeScript plugins is similar to dealing with npm packages in Node.js or front-end web development.

Finding Plugins

The NativeScript team runs an official marketplace, which offers a filtered list of npm plugins connected to NativeScript. All plugins featured in the marketplace come with information that describes their quality. A search for "accelerometer" on the plugins marketplace will lead us to the required plugin.

Alternatively, because NativeScript plugins are npm packages, we may locate NativeScript plugins by searching for "nativescript-plugin-name" on npm's homepage. For example, a search for "nativescript accelerometer" will direct us to the NativeScript accelerometer plugin.

If we can't find a plugin, you can always ask for help on Stack Overflow. The NativeScript team and community may be able to assist us in locating what we are searching for.

Also, check over the NativeScript core modules, shipped as a dependency with every NativeScript project. There's a chance the functionality we want is already built-in. If we still can't find what we're looking for, we may post a request for the plugin as an idea in the NativeScript community forum or try our hand at building it.

Installing Plugins

Once we've identified the plugin we're looking for, use the tns plugin add command to include it into our project:

```
tns plugin add <pluginname>
```

The following command, for example, installs the NativeScript camera plugin:

```
tns plugin add @nativescript/camera
```

We may also use the NPM command npm install instead of the NativeScript CLI command plugin add if we like:

```
npm i @nativescript/camera -save
```

The installation of a NativeScript plugin is similar to that of a npm package. The NativeScript CLI gets the plugin from npm and places it in our project's root node modules folder. The NativeScript CLI adds the plugin to our project's root package.json file and resolves the plugin's dependencies throughout this process.

Installing Plugins as Developer Dependencies

The command tns plugin add, as described above, is performing npm i --save behind the scenes. If we need to install a developer dependent (e.g., @nativescript/types or @nativescript/webpack), we must explicitly save it as a devDependency. Use the npm install command with the --save-dev parameter to do this. As an example:

```
npm i @nativescript/types --save-dev
```

The distinction between dependencies and developer dependencies is that dependencies are necessary for running, whereas devDependencies are only required during development. As an example of dependence, consider the @nativescript/camera plugin, which is needed at runtime to access the hardware camera. The @nativescript/types, on the other hand, is a developer dependency that is only necessary for intelliSense during the development process. The devDependencies should not be installed as dependents (large application size) to prevent massive output build files. We can find an example package.json file that uses both dependencies and devDependencies here.

Importing and Using Plugins

After installing the required plugin, you may begin utilizing it in our project. It should be noted that each plugin may have its setup requirements; therefore, always read the plugin's instructions and the README file thoroughly. The code sample below demonstrates the fundamentals of the @nativescript/camera plugin.

```
import { requestPermissions } from "@nativescript/
camera";
requestPermissions();
```

Removing Plugins

Run the following command from the command line to delete a NativeScript plugin from our project:

```
tns plugin remove <pluginname>
```

The following command, for example, removes the NativeScript camera plugin:

```
tns plugin remove @nativescript/camera
```

The removal of a NativeScript plugin is similar to the removal of an npm package.

The NativeScript CLI deletes any plugin files from our app's node modules folder in the project's root. The CLI also removes any plugin dependencies and the plugin from the root package.json file of our project.

The removal of a NativeScript plugin is similar to the removal of an npm package.

The NativeScript CLI deletes any plugin files from our app's node modules folder in the project's root. The CLI also removes any plugin dependencies and the plugin from the root package.json file of our project.

In this chapter, we covered Angular in NativeScript. We learned how to create a Web and Mobile and upgrade our project by using Angular 10. We also covered data binding in NativeScript, as well as plugins.

CHAPTER 5

Digging Deeper

IN THIS CHAPTER

> ➤ Android emulator tips

> ➤ Custom webpack configuration

> ➤ Creating custom UI controls

> ➤ Styling

> ➤ NativeScript Conventions

In the previous chapter, we learned how to create an App with Angular and Angular components and routing, and we also covered Angular data binding, services, and plugins. This chapter covers the Android emulator, UI controls, styling and convention, as well as CLI in NativeScript.

INSTALL ANDROID EMULATORS

Aside from utilizing genuine Android devices, downloading, installing, and using an Android emulator is a feasible option. All Android emulators that are connected and identified by the tns device command can be used in NativeScript. This command's details may be found in the tns device section.

Tip: Emulators sometimes take a while to boot up. Start the emulator before performing other CLI commands as a best practice and to minimize timing difficulties. After starting the emulator, leave it open to avoid the initial load time when we need to deploy an Android application.

DOI: 10.1201/9781003299394-5

Creating an Android Virtual Device in Android Studio

Follow the official guidelines on Creating and Managing Virtual Devices, which cover the process of downloading, installing, and utilizing Android Emulators in Android Studio.

Note: If our top-level "Tools" menu lacks the "Android" option (a common problem in versions >3.0.0), follow the instructions in this Stack Overflow answer to add it to the toolbar and activate the AVD Manager.

Using a Command-Line Tool to Create an Android Virtual Device

The avdmanager is a command-line program for creating and managing Android Virtual Devices (AVDs). The avdmanager utility is included in the Android SDK Tools package (25.3.0 and above) and may be found at ANDROID HOME PATH HERE>/tools/bin/. See the official avdmanager documentation for further information on the avdmanager and how to use it to build AVDs.

To build a new AVD, use the following command syntax:

```
$ cd $ANDROID_HOME/tools/bin
$ avdmanager create avd -n name -k "sdk_id" [-c
{path|size}] [-f] [-p path]
```

We must give the AVD a name and indicate the ID of the SDK package to use for the AVD using sdk_id enclosed in quotes. The following command, for example, builds an AVD called test using the x86 system image for API level 25:

```
avdmanager create avd -n test -k
"system-images;android-25;google_apis;x86"
```

It should be noted that the command indicates that the system image has already been downloaded. Use the sdkmanager to download an image. sdkmanager "system-images;android-25;google apis;x86" is an example.

The following illustrates how to use the other options: -c path|size: the path to this AVD's SD card image or the size of a new SD card image to generate for this AVD, in KB or MB, represented by K or M. -c path/to/sdcard/, for example, or -c 1000M. -f: force the AVD to be created. Use this option if we need to replace an existing AVD with a new AVD with the same name. -p path: the path to the directory where the files for this AVD will be produced. If no path is specified, the AVD will be produced under ~/.android/avd/.

The list command may be used to display a list of all the downloaded system images.

```
avdmanager list
```

CUSTOM webpack CONFIGURATION

What Exactly Is webpack Configuration?

The webpack configuration file webpack.config.js provides all of the configuration, plugins, loaders, and required to generate the JavaScript portion of the NativeScript application. The file resides in the NativeScript application's root directory. The content of the file vary for each flavor (Angular, Vue.js, React, TypeScript, JavaScript) because the way the files are processed in the application differs. The default configuration file comes from the @nativescript/webpack plugin during its postinstall stage (or when we run the update-ns-webpack --configs script found in your project dir>/ node modules/.bin/directory).

We are continuously working to enhance the content of the default webpack.config.js files; therefore, we implemented a check to see if our application's webpack.config.js file varies from the new default one and show a warning if it does. However, we'll need to add some specific logic to our webpack.config.js file in many circumstances, such as if we have particular files to transfer or custom Android activity. In this situation, the above warning will appear every time we update @nativescript/webpack. Also, if we want to ensure that we have all of the essential modifications from the default webpack.config.js that comes with the new version of @nativescript/webpack, we must manually combine the two webpack settings.

How to Use Custom webpack Configuration

We may use a custom path to webpack settings starting with NativeScript v6.4.0 and @nativescript/webpack v1.5.0. To achieve this we need to set webpackConfigPath property in our nsconfig.json file:

Set in nsconfig.json

```
{
    "webpackConfigPath": "./my-custom.webpack.config.js"
}
```

Create the real file my-custom.webpack.config.js in the application's root directory (as specified in nsconfig.json). We can put custom logic in this file.

First Example:

```
const webpackConfig = require("./webpack.config");
module.exports = (env) => {
    // Here we can modify env before passing them
to the default config
    const config = webpackConfig(env);

    // Here, we can modify everything created by
the default configuration
    return config;
}
```

Note: Although we are not required to utilize the default webpack.config.js file, we highly advise that. It includes the basic rules and logic for converting our application scripts into NativeScript applications.

Execute the build/run operation to ensure that everything works as expected:

```
$ tns run <platform>
```

[Optional] Delete webpack.config.js from our application and put it to.gitignore – If we no longer want to see the warnings for different webpack settings, we may safely remove webpack.config.js from our application and add it to our .gitignore file, where no one will commit it. As a result, during dependency installation, the @nativescript/webpack postinstall script will always insert the current default configuration file. If we want to review all changes while updating the webpack.config.js file, we may still commit it to our repository with the default content and avoid this step.

Second Example: It explains how to utilize custom webpack configuration files.

Add new assets to the list of assets to be copied:

If we wish to add more assets to our application, we may do so using the following method:

```
const webpackConfig = require("./webpack.config");
const CopyWebpackPlugin =
require("copy-webpack-plugin");
module.exports = env => {
    const config = webpackConfig(env);
    const customCopyInstance = new CopyWebpackPlugin([
        { from: { glob: "my-custom-dir/**" } },
    ]);
    config.plugins.unshift(customCopyInstance);
    return config;
};
```

In this situation, we add a new CopyWebpackPlugin instance that will copy all files from our my-custom-dir directory to the build folder.

Custom Application and Activity (Android)

We may accomplish the following if we have a custom application and activity for Android:

```
const webpackConfig = require("./webpack.config");
const path = require("path");
module.exports = env => {
    env = env || {};
    env.appComponents = env.appComponents || [];
    env.appComponents.push(path.resolve(__dirname,
"app", "activity.android.ts"));
    env.entries = env.entries || {};
    env.entries.application = "./application.android";
    const config = webpackConfig(env);
    return config;
};
```

Note: In this example, our activity code is located in the app directory, in the file activity.android.ts. The application may be found in the app directory, in the application.android.ts file.

Add More Rules for Specific Files

If we wish to have some files processed further:

```
const webpackConfig = require("./webpack.config");
const path = require("path");
module.exports = env => {
    const config = webpackConfig(env);
    const babelOptions = {
        babelrc: false,
        presets: [
            "@babel/preset-react"
        ],
        plugins: [ ]
    };
    config.module.rules.push(
        {
            test: /\.js(x?)$/,
            exclude: /node_modules/,
            use: {
                loader: "babel-loader",
                options: babelOptions
            },
        }
    );
    config.resolve.extensions = [".js", ".jsx",
".scss", ".css"];
    return config;
};
```

Delete the Default Plugin

In some instances, we may wish to delete some of the preset plugins that the default setup includes:

```
const webpackConfig = require("./webpack.config");
const path = require("path");
module.exports = env => {
    env = env || {};
    const config = webpackConfig(env);
    if (env.ios) {
        config.plugins = config.plugins.filter
(p => !(p && p.constructor && p.constructor.name ===
"HotModuleReplacementPlugin"));
    }
    return config;
};
```

In this example, we show how to deactivate the HotModuleReplacement Plugin plugin while developing for iOS.

iOS APP EXTENSIONS

iOS App extensions allow users to access the app's functionality and content from anywhere on iOS. App extensions allow users to engage with other programs while also accessing the app's functionality without launching it. There are over 25 distinct App extensions templates in the most recent version of XCode. They encompass sharing, photo editing, file system access, widgets, custom alerts, actions, custom keyboards, and many other features. Each extension is a component of the app, but they also function independently.

NativeScript App Extensions

NativeScript CLI 5.3.0 included Beta support for iOS App extensions. While the extension should be created and developed in Xcode (using Objective-C), the resulting files can be integrated into an existing NativeScript app via a plugin (that contains the extension) or directly by introducing the extension files in a separate folder named the extension inside/App_Resources/iOS/extensions/.

For example, if we have a TestExtension extension, the extension files should be stored under/App_Resources/iOS/extensions/TestExtension.

Including an App Extension in an Existing Application
Prerequisites:

- The App extension that was generated.
- Pre-existing NativeScript applications, we may use the create command to construct a basic application for testing purposes.

```
tns create today-extension --tsc
```

To incorporate the App extension, follow these steps:

1. Create a folder called extensions in /app/App_Resources/iOS/.

2. Create a primary folder in the extensions folder that includes the extension files. Create a folder called TestExtension that contains all of the extension files, for example.

3. Create a file named extension.json in the TestExtension folder (where the extension files are stored). This configuration file specifies the SDK frameworks used in the extension (through the frameworks key) and the optional image resources used for the extension icon (via assetcatalogCompilerAppiconName key).

As an example:

```
{
    "frameworks": ["NotificationCenter
.framework"],
    "assetcatalogCompilerAppiconName":
"AppIconExtension"
}
```

frameworks is a key with an array of framework names as the value.

assetcatalogCompilerAppiconName key – the value is the name of the .appiconset from the .xcassets catalogue within the extension folder – (AppIconExtension.appiconset in the example above).

4. Rebuild the program, and our extension should be ready to use.

Adding an App Extension to a Plugin

The method for adding an App extension to a plugin is the same as stated above, with the exception that the extension is stored in a different location. Create the extensions folder (along with all associated files) under our plugin's platforms/ios folder.

iOS WatchOS Applications

With version 5.4, the NativeScript CLI adds Beta support for integrating a WatchOS application in your NativeScript-created iOS mobile app.

Basic requirements:

- NativeScript CLI versions 5.4 and above are supported

- The NativeScript project

- Xcode 10 and later

- Devices that have been paired or simulated (iPhone and iWatch running WatchOS 4.x/5.x or above)

Keep in mind that the default Watch App produced with Xcode will not operate with WatchOS 4.x. WATCHOS DEPLOYMENT TARGET must be explicitly specified in the configuration json by the user.

- Objective-C was used to construct the WatchOS app (Swift code is not supported yet).

NativeScript Application for WatchOS

Execute the following steps to incorporate your current WatchOS application into your NativeScript project:

- Using Xcode, create a Single View App.
- Add a target for a watch app by going to File > New > Target > WatchKit App.
- Give our watch app a name, such as MyFirstWatchApp. Verify that Objective-C is selected as our language on the same screen.

Note: We can skip steps 1–3 if our Watch app is already created.

- Copy the MyFirstWatchApp and MyFirstWatchAppExtension files to.../apps/MyApp/app/App_Resources/iOS/watchapp/MyFirst WatchApp and.../apps/MyApp/app/App_Resources/iOS/watchextension/ MyFirstWatchAppExtension, respectively.
- Replace the value of WKCompanionAppBundleIdentifier in the Watch App's Info.plist with $(WK_APP_BUNDLE_IDENTIFIER).
- Replace WKAppBundleIdentifier with $(WK_APP_BUNDLE_ IDENTIFIER) in the Watch Extension's Info.plist.
- We may populate the Watch App's Assets.xcassets and add the appiconset's name to the .../apps/MyApp/app/App_Resources/iOS/ watchapp/MyFirstWatchApp/watchapp.json.

```
{
    "assetcatalogCompilerAppiconName": "AppIcon"
}
```

- We may change the WATCHOS_DEPLOYMENT_TARGET of the Watch App by adding the following value to the _watchapp.json_ file:

```
{
    "assetcatalogCompilerAppiconName": "AppIcon",
    "targetBuildConfigurationProperties": {
        "WATCHOS_DEPLOYMENT_TARGET": 4.1
    }
}
```

- Create and run the NativeScript application

```
tns run ios
```

- The application will be installed and launched on our iOS device/ simulator. Ascertain if the test iPhone is already linked to the test iWatch. When the iOS app is launched, the Watch app is instantly installed on the testing iWatch device.

USING JavaScript TO ACCESS NATIVE APIs

In this part, we'll go through the fundamentals of using JavaScript to access native APIs. This section focuses on how basic types are mapped between JavaScript and the relevant native platform. After that, we'll go through how complicated things are represented and accessed. Finally, we discuss TypeScript and the @nativescript/types add-on, which provide TypeScript definitions for both the Android and iOS development platforms.

NativeScript provides access to all native APIs provided by the under-lying platform. Many things happen behind the scenes to produce this behavior. One of these is marshaling, which is transferring JavaScript and Objective-C data types for iOS to Java data types for Android.

This section will teach us how to use JavaScript to access native APIs with various data type arguments.

Numeric Types

All native numeric types (e.g., char, short, int, double, float on iOS and byte, short, int, long, double, float on Android) are implicitly transformed to JavaScript numbers and vice versa. For example, on iOS, run the following code:

- **iOS**

```
console.log('pow(3.5, 4) = ${pow(3.5, 4)}');
```

The JavaScript number literals are converted to native doubles by the iOS Runtime and sent to the native pow(double x, double y) function. The native integer that is returned is automatically translated to a JavaScript number and supplied to console.log (). The same holds true for Android.

- **Android**

```
console.log('min(4, 5) = ${java.lang.Math.
min(4, 5)}');
```

The java.lang.Math.min() function takes two numbers as input. The Android Runtime recognizes the function signature java.lang.Math.min() and converts literals 4 and 5 to their Java integer data type representation. In addition, the returned integer is immediately converted to a JavaScript number and provided to console.log ().

String

Strings in JavaScript are implicitly marshalled to java.lang. String on Android is equivalent to NSString on iOS, and vice versa.

- **iOS**

```
let button = new UIButton();
button.setTitleForState('Button title',
UIControlStateNormal); // 'Button title' converted
to NSString
console.log(button.titleLabel.text); // returned
NSString is converted to JavaScript string
```

- **Android**

```
const file = new java.io.File('myfile.txt');
// 'myfile.txt' converted to java.lang.String
```

The methods on NSString classes that are stated as returning instancetype – init and factory methods are an exception. This implies that in Objective-C, a call to NSString.stringWithString with the return type instancetype will return a wrapper over an NSString instance rather than a JavaScript string.

Exception: Methods on NSString classes marked as returning instancetype constitute an exception (e.g., init methods and factory methods). Calls to NSString.stringWithString, for example, return instancetype in Objective-C. Such calls will return a wrapper over an NSString object rather than a JavaScript string in our NativeScript code.

Boolean

On Android, boolean values are implicitly marshalled to boolean and BOOL on iOS, and vice versa.

- **iOS**

```
let str = NSString.stringWithString('YES');
let isTrue = str.boolValue();
```

- **Android**

```
let str = new java.lang.String('Hello everyone');
let result = str.endsWith(' everyone ');
console.log(result); // true
```

Array

JavaScript arrays on Android correspond to specialized Java arrays and NSArray on iOS.

- **iOS**

```
let nsArray = NSArray.arrayWithArray(['Fours',
'Fives', 'Twos', 'Sevens']);
let jsArray = ['Ones', 'Twos', 'Threes']; // pure
- JavaScript array
let firstCommon = nsArray.firstObjectCommonWithArr
ay(jsArray);
console.log(firstCommon); // Twos
```

- **Android**

The code shows how to call an ns.example.Math.minElement(int[] array) from JavaScript:

```
let numbers = [4, 5, 18, -2, 5, 7];
let min = ns.example.Math.minElement(numbers); // -2
```

Class and Object

A constructor represents all native classes in the JavaScript environment. Every static method on a native class becomes a function on its JavaScript constructor function, and every instance method becomes a function on the JavaScript prototype. Although relatively simple, instantiating objects and invoking JavaScript functions have specific nuances (especially on iOS), discussed more below.

Using Classes and Objects on iOS

An example of how to create and consume an instance of the NSMutableArray class in JavaScript:

```
let array = new NSMutableArray();
array.addObject(new NSObject());
```

This code sample creates an NSMutableArray instance and adds an object using the addObject(object) function. Here's what happens behind the scenes: The iOS Runtime converts the new NSMutableArray() function to a [[NSMutableArray alloc] init] call. This instance is then encapsulated in a JavaScript object and saved in the array variable. It has in its prototype chain all public properties and methods accessible by NSMutableArray (and its parent classes). While calling addObject(object) is easy, calling Objective-C methods with more parameters follows a set of basic rules that determine how Objective-C selectors are mapped to JavaScript functions. Take a look at the following NSMutableArray selector: replaceObjectsInRange:withObjectsFromArray:range:. It is represented in JavaScript by the following function:

Replace ObjectsInRangeWith ObjectsFromArrayRange(objectsToRange, sourceArray, sourceRange) (argument names are arbitrary). It is worth noting that the function name is formed by attaching the names of the arguments as defined by the Objective-C selector, beginning with a small letter for the first argument and ending with a capital letter for each consecutive argument.

NSDictionary

We will very certainly come across methods that take NSDictionary objects as arguments. There are just a few ways to make an NSDictionary instance:

- Using NSDictionary and arrays to transmit keys and values.

```
let dict = new NSDictionary([".example.com",
"cookieName", "/", "cookieValue"],
[NSHTTPCookieDomain, NSHTTPCookieName, NSHTTPCooki
ePath,NSHTTPCookieValue]);
let cookie = NSHTTPCookie.
cookieWithProperties(dict);
```

- Using JSON literals

```
let cookie = NSHTTPCookie.cookieWithProperties({ [N
SHTTPCookieDomain]:".example.com", [NSHTTPCookieNa
me]:"cookieName", [NSHTTPCookiePath]:"/", [NSHTTPC
ookieValue]:"cookieValue"});
```

In the second example, we send the method a JSON literal. NSHTTPCookieDomain is a variable, and we must use a calculated property name to acquire its value (otherwise, we are getting "NSHTTPCookieDomain" as key).

On Android, we may work with classes and objects:

The code demonstrates how an instance of the android.widget.Button is created in JavaScript:

```
let context = ...;
let button = new android.widget.Button(context);
button.setText("My Button");
```

As we can see, the native Java types are made available via their respective packages. In other words, to access a native Java type, you merely need to know and explicitly mention the package in which it is housed. Native Java methods are accessible in the same manner as standard JavaScript methods: invoking the method identifier and passing in the necessary parameters.

Undefined and Null

Undefined and Null in JavaScript correspond to the Java null pointer and nil in Objective-C. Native null values correspond to JavaScript null values.

- **iOS**

```
console.log(NSStringFromClass(null));
```

- **Android**

```
let context = ...;
const button = new android.widget.Button(context);
button.setOnClickListener(undefined);
```

TypeScript via IntelliSense and Access to Native APIs

To get access and Intellisense for native APIs, we must add a developer dependency to @nativescript/types.

Install and enable steps:

- **npm install @nativescript/types --save-dev**

  Note: To prevent including the tremendously large declaration files in the output build file, always install the plugin as a devDependency (npm I @nativescript/types --save-dev option).

  In the root project directory, create reference.d.ts and add the following:

  ```
  /// <reference path="node_modules/@nativescript/
  types/index.d.ts" />
  ```

  The file android.d.ts comes with typings produced for API level 17 by default. We may require access to a newer API level's class, method, or property as an Android developer. The @nativescript/types plugin includes produced typings for all API levels 17 through 27 and associated typings from the relevant support library. To utilize typings for a specific Android level, replace the reference to the default declaration file with the one we choose. The files for each API level are prefixed with a dash followed by the API level number (e.g., for API 21 the file is named android-21.d.ts).

  Assume we're constructing an API 21+ application and we require typings created for that API level:

  ```
  /// <reference path="node_modules/@nativescript/
  types-android/lib/android-21.d.ts" />
  ```

  Note: Caution should be exercised while utilizing newer API level functions. The program will crash if we try to utilize a class, method, or property from a higher API level on a lower API level device.

- **Change the following values in tsconfig.json:**

  ```
  {
    "compilerOptions": {
      ...
      "module": "esnext",
      "target": "es2015",
      "moduleResolution": "node",
      "lib": ["es2018", "dom"],
  }
  ```

  It should be noted that d.ts files take a significant amount of memory and CPU power. Consider adding the option skipLibCheck to tsconfig.json.

METADATA

Both NativeScript runtimes require metadata to allow JavaScript code to invoke native iOS or Android code. It contains all of the necessary information about each of the supported native classes, interfaces, protocols, structures, enumerations, functions, variables, and so on. It is created at build time by inspecting the native libraries from the SDKs for the Android and iOS operating systems, and any third-party libraries and frameworks that the N application employs.

Metadata Filtering

NativeScript contains all supported entities in the metadata by default. This enables app and plugin developers to use JavaScript to call any native API. While it is useful during development, having information for all APIs is not always ideal. There may be security problems; runtime performance may suffer (due to a bigger metabase that must be queried when an unfamiliar item is encountered or at startup); or app size may rise owing to needless metadata that is never utilized.

There is support for blacklisting and whitelisting symbols by their native name, giving developers control over what is or is not included in the output data.

Metadata Filtering rules in plugins:

Plugins can specify their list of APIs that are called from JavaScript in a file called native-api-usage.json, which can be found in each platform directory (platforms/android or platforms/ios). It follows the same format as:

```
{
    "uses": [
      "java.util:List"
    ]
}
```

Metadata Filtering rules in apps:

Applications have the last say on what metadata filtering will be used. They supply native-api-usage.json files with the following format, which may be found in App_Resources/Android and App_Resources/iOS:

```
{
    "whitelist-plugins-usages": true,
    "whitelist": [
        "java.util:Base64*"
    ],
```

```
    "blacklist": [
        "java.util:Locale*"
    ]
}
```

Rule Syntax

Each list is made up of pattern items that share the following characteristics:

The <pattern1>[:pattern2] format is used for entries.

Pattern1 is matched against Java package names on Android, whereas matched pattern2--against classes, interfaces, and enums.

On iOS, pattern1 matches Clang module/submodule names, whereas matched pattern2--structs, global functions, enums, Objective-C interfaces, protocols, categories, constants, and so on.

Wildcards ("*": - any number of characters and "?": - any single character) are supported in patterns.

An unnamed or empty pattern is equal to being set to "*." (matching everything).

Rule Semantics

After assessing a platform's filtering criteria, N CLI generates final whitelist and blacklist files in the native project for use by the corresponding metadata generator. The blacklist is always the same as the one set by the app. While the flag whitelist-plugins-usages determine the whitelist:

- If this is correct, the final whitelist is a concatenation of the use lists of all plugins and the app's whitelist.

- Otherwise, it is equivalent to the whitelist of the app.

These two lists unambiguously dictate how filtering is carried out:

- If the whitelist is empty, everything is assumed to be whitelisted by default.

- Only entities that match a rule are deemed whitelisted if it contains at least one rule.

- All entities that are not whitelisted or that meet a rule on the blacklist are removed from metadata.

- The metadata includes all other entities.

Troubleshooting

Missing metadata entities may cause runtime errors. For example, if a native class is mistakenly filtered out; its constructor method will be undefined, resulting in an exception when it is invoked. Because the reasons for something being undefined might vary, determining what the reason is can be challenging. After a successful build, investigate the metadata generator's verbose logs to see whether metadata filtering is to blame:

- On iOS, look for platforms/ios/build/<configuration>-<platform>/ metadata-generation-stderr-<arch>.txt (e.g., platforms/ios/build/ Debug-iphonesimulator/metadata-generation-stderr-x86_64.txt).

- They may be found in platforms/android/build-tools/buildMetadata. log on Android.

- For each global symbol detected by the generator, there should be a line indicating whether it was included in metadata or not and whether rules or exceptions resulted in this.

Examples:

- **verbose:** Blacklisted kCFBuddhistCalendar from CoreFoundation. CFLocale (disabled by 'CoreFoundation*:*') – when no whitelist rules exist, a blacklisted symbol will display only the rule that disabled it.

- **verbose:** Blacklisted NSString from Foundation.NSString – Some blacklisted symbols will not define a rule when at least one whitelist rule. This signifies that the symbol did not meet any of the whitelist criteria.

- **verbose:** Blacklisted PHImageContentModeDefault from Photos. PhotosTypes (enabled by 'Photos.PhotosTypes:*', disabled by 'Photos. PhotosTypes:PHImageContentMode*').

- **verbose:** Blacklisted String from java.lang (enabled by java.lang:*, disabled by java.lang:String) – Blacklisted entry that meets both whitelist rule and blacklist rule will be specified in both cases.

- **verbose:** It included NSObject from ObjectiveC.NSObject – When there's no whitelist rules, an included symbol will not identify the rule that allowed to be included.

- **verbose:** Included PHCollectionListType from Photos.PhotosTypes (enabled by 'Photos.PhotosTypes:*').

- **verbose:** It included StrictMath from java.lang (enabled by java. lang:*) – When symbol can be included because it matched a rule as from whitelist (but not any from the blacklist), that rule is printed.

- **verbose:** Exception [Name: 'vfwprintf', JsName: 'vfwprintf', Module: 'Darwin.C.wchar', File: '/Applications/Xcode.app/Contents/ Developer/Platforms/iPhoneSimulator.platform/Developer/SDKs/ iPhoneSimulator13.2.sdk/usr/include/wchar.h']: It Can't create type dependency. –> [Type Decayed]: It Can't create type dependency. –> [Type Typedef]: The VaList type is not supported. – If symbol is not included because it is not supported for whatever reason, the logged error will mention this. Because {N} does not permit calling functions with variable parameter lists, the symbol cannot be utilized from JavaScript in this circumstance.

- **verbose:** Exception [Name: 'GLKVector3Make', JsName: 'GLKVector3Make', Module:'GLKit.GLKVector3', File:'/Applications/ Xcode.app/Contents/Developer/Platforms/iPhoneSimulator.plat- form/Developer/SDKs/iPhoneSimulator13.2.sdk/System/Library/ Frameworks/GLKit.framework/Headers/GLKVector3.h']: Can't cre- ate type dependency. –> [Type Typedef]: It Can't create type depen- dency. –> [Type Elaborated]: Can't create type dependency. –> [Type Record]: The record is a union – More example of an unsupported symbol, this time because unions are not supported.

MEMORY MANAGEMENT

NativeScript enables the execution of JavaScript code from native code and vice versa. It does this by constructing bridge counterparts for each instance exposed to the "other world" (native or JavaScript). These allow JavaScript developers to access and consume native APIs by: * implement- ing native interfaces or inheriting from native classes in JavaScript * creat- ing and accessing native instances and calling into their functions from JavaScript.

In this part, we discuss the life cycle of JavaScript and native instances and certain problematic possibilities that may develop as a result of the complexities of having two garbage-collected runtimes (Android) or a garbage-collected runtime and reference counting (iOS).

- Terms

- iOS

- Android

- Common tips

Terms

- **Disclaimer:** These terminologies are not necessarily well established in the literature, but we present them in the following sections for your convenience.

- **Native instance:** Objective-C class instance (iOS) or Java class instance (Android).

- **Reference counting:** The Objective-C runtime in iOS employs reference counting for lifetime management. Instances retain a counter that can be increased and decremented internally. The instance's reference count is increased each time a strong reference is set to point to it. When a strong reference is updated, the reference count of the previous instance it referenced to is decremented. When the count hits zero, the instance is deallocated.

- **GC:** It stands for garbage collection in general. When the GC runs, it first blocks all threads to discover all strong instances on the stack. The execution then precedes until the GC tags all accessible objects in a separate thread. The threads are then blocked again to complete the marking. Finally, it finalizes and deallocates any discovered unreachable instances. While the real GC mechanism may be far more advanced, all implementations in virtual machines used for UI attempt to keep the main thread stopped as little as possible. NativeScript uses three state-of-the-art virtual machines with garbage collectors: the Android Java VM, Android's V8, and iOS's JavaScriptCore.

- **Weak/strong reference:** Instances can make weak or strong references to one another. When there's a path in the graph of strong references from one instance to another (one held by a local variable on the stack, a static field, etc.), the second instance cannot be garbage collected. Weak references, however, they do not obstruct the gathering of their referent.

- **Splice:** Let's introduce a new NativeScript term: splice. A splice is a link formed between a native instance and its JavaScript equivalent by a JavaScript instance. In certain circumstances, the splice may be instantiated in native first (e.g., the iOS AppDelegate class, Android's Application, Activity, and Fragment classes).

The splices include a reference to both a JavaScript and a native instance:

- If the splice has a solid reference to an instance, it will prevent the GC from collecting it.

- If the splice contains a weak reference to an instance that is normally unreachable, that instance can be collected.

- If both JavaScript and native instances are collected, the splice will be deallocated.

- While any one of its instances is alive and the other one is dead, the splice will be half-dead.

The splices display the following characteristics:

- Return the native instance of a JavaScript instance.

- Get the JavaScript instance from a native instance.

- Synchronize the two instances' life cycles.

- Method calls to and from JavaScript and native instances are proxy.

- When methods are invoked while in a half-dead state, throw exceptions.

A splice is created:

- A splice is produced when a native instance is returned from a constructor, method, property, block, anonymous interface, lambda, or any JavaScript function.

- When a native instance is supplied as an argument to a JavaScript constructor, method, property, block, anonymous interface, lambda, and so on.

- When a JavaScript-extended native class is instantiated in either native or JavaScript.

iOS

The Objective-C runtime lacks a garbage collector and instead depends on reference counting. The iOS runtime intercepts the retain and release calls of each Objective-C object. The Objective-C association API allows native objects to be dynamically given key-value pairs. JavaScriptCore provides an API for protecting JavaScript instances, which may be used to make them strong or weak (i.e., allow or deny them from being garbage collected). The word "splice" refers to the process of connecting an Objective-C instance of a class to a JavaScript instance.

Splice LifeCycle

A splice increases the ref-count of the Objective-C instance by one, and if the ref-count is more significant than one, the splice makes the JavaScript instance strong. From that moment forward:

- When the Objective-C instance ref-count increases from 1 to 2, the splice strengthens its weak reference to the JavaScript instance.

- If the Objective-C instance ref-count is reduced from 2 to 1, the splice converts its strong reference to the JavaScript instance to a weak reference.

- Only when the ref-count of the Objective-C instance is one will the splice have a weak reference to the JavaScript instance, making the JavaScript instance suitable for trash collection. If the GC cannot contact this JavaScript instance from an alive JavaScript object, it will mark it for collection. After that, when JSC finalizes the JavaScript instance, the splice will schedule a decrementation of the Objective-C instance's ref-count, finally deallocating it and disposing of the splice.

Implementation Characteristics

1. **Native Instances Can Easily Leak:** Because the JavaScript GC does not traverse native objects and fails to detect cycles, we may create a reference cycle in Objective-C that leaks native and JavaScript instances. Native tools (such as Xcode and Instruments) may be used to detect and locate leaking instances.

2. **Native Instances Might Be Deallocated Prematurely:** We can allow instances to be prematurely collected when utilizing weak properties or APIs that include methods like setTarget:selector:... They add the Objective-C instance as a native target, but only via a weak Objective-C reference that does not increase the ref-count of the Objective-C instance. When the target ref-count stays 1, and the JavaScript GC collects the JavaScript instance of the splice, the Objective-C instance is likewise deallocated. The frustrating aspect is that the code works most of the time correctly. Still, owing to the non-deterministic completion of the GC, it will occasionally cause the aforementioned deallocation and cause the application to raise an exception or crash.

3. **Half-Dead Splice:** The native Objective-C object is scheduled for deallocation when the JavaScript equivalent of a splice is collected. The native instance has a relatively short time window in which a message may be submitted (e.g., a method call on a delegate normally held in a weakref property). This will result in a call to a JavaScript instance that has already been collected.

4. **Extremely Objective-C Friendly:** The implementation is very Objective-C friendly and predictable overall. Working with native APIs necessitates more attention to memory management, but nothing more than normal iOS understanding. It is incredibly user-friendly and does not cause interruptions in the main UI thread.

5. **Deep Hierarchies Die Hard:** Based on number of nodes in the list, the amount of GC cycles required to collect a linked list exposed from Objective-C to JavaScript is linear.

   Consider the following scenario (which is based on a genuine problem handled in @nativescript/core):

```
Page           ->           StackPanel -> Button
|.ios                       |.ios       |.ios
UIViewController            UIView        UIButton
```

When set to "Visible," the UIViewController's root view property points to the UIView, which contains a collection containing a reference to the UIButton. Each one has its JavaScript wrapper. While the visual tree is displayed, the Objective-C UIViewController, UIView, and UIButton have reference counts of two. The JavaScript references are "protected" (which means that the JavaScript GC will consider these objects to be rooted and will not collect them).

When user Navigates Away from page, the parent UINavigationController will delete the UIViewController and reduce its reference count to one, "unprotecting" its JavaScript wrapper and making it trash collection-eligible.

The next GC then collects the Page, but the UIView still has a reference count of 2 and its JavaScript wrapper is protected.

Android

The Java and JavaScript VMs in Android are both GC-based. For subscribing to GC events, the Android Java VM provides a restricted public API. In contrast, the V8 has a richer API for subscribing to GC prologue and epilogue, as well as notifications when a JavaScript instance is marked for collection, allowing us to optionally revive it if we discover that it is still being referenced from outside.

Splice LifeCycle

The Android splice comes in three varieties:

- When a splice is formed for an "anonymous interface," such as new ClickListener({...}), it is deemed to "have implementation object."

- For a "extended native class," such as var MyView = View.extends({...}); var MyView = new MyView();, a splice is formed.

- When a splice is made for var button = new android.widget, it is regarded as not "having implementation object."

- Button(...) for instantiating a native class.

- When a Java instance is returned by the getValue() method, a splice is produced for val i = anAndroidObject.getValue().

When a splice is constructed: It has a strong reference to the Java instance, which the Android Java VM GC cannot collect.

On the V8 GC collection phase: All additional accessible JavaScript instances will be explored from the JavaScript instances of any splice that has an implementation object. For each of these JavaScript objects that may be accessed:

- If the object reached is an implementation object, the splice will be tagged as "implementation reachable."

- Otherwise, it will be ignored.

Following that, all splices are handled in the following order:

- Suppose a JavaScript instance is designated for collection but does not have an implementation object. In that case, the JavaScript instance is left to be collected, and the reference to the Java instance is made weak.

- If the JavaScript instance is designated for collection, contains an implementation object, and is weakly referenced, The JavaScript instance is revived if the Java object is alive.

  - If the Java object is no longer alive, the JavaScript instance is left to collect.

  - If a JavaScript instance is tagged for collection, contains an implementation object, and is strongly referred to, the JavaScript instance of the splice is resurrected.

- If the splice was not tagged "implementation accessible" in the preceding phase, the reference to its Java instance is rendered weak.

  - The splice's JavaScript instance is resurrected.

  - If the splice was not tagged "implementation accessible" in the preceding phase, the reference to its Java instance is rendered weak.

Implementation Characteristics
Premature Collection
Unlike iOS, the Android runtime manages both Java and JavaScript. Because the native framework rarely utilizes weak references, premature

collection is rarely seen. Half-dead splices are the most typical problem with GC for Android.

Leaks

Memory leaks are uncommon. Suppose there is a pool of unreachable splices from Java or JavaScript. In that case, the V8 GC will tell the JavaScript instances that they are designated for collection at some time, and the reference to the Java equivalent will be rendered weak. The following Android VM GC will collect the Java instances, followed by the V8 GC, which will collect the JavaScript instances (because the Java counterparts will be dead).

Half-Dead Splice

Because garbage collectors drive collection, it is feasible to keep a weak reference to the JavaScript instance of a splice. The splice can reference the Java instance weak after a V8 GC, allowing the Android VM GC to collect it. Then, if the JavaScript instance is acquired through the weak reference and its methods are accessed before the next V8 GC, it will access a half-dead splice (since the Java counterpart is dead already). The runtime error indicates that we were unable to locate an object with the supplied id. These issues are seen as random and are difficult to replicate.

Splices Die Fast

Several splices and JavaScript instances can be produced; however, properties may be lost.

JavaScript instances may be easily retrieved from splices that lack an implementation object. Consider the following execution sequence:

- In JavaScript, a splice is constructed by obtaining an existing Java instance.

- It is used for some work, and new JavaScript properties are assigned to it.

- The JavaScript instance reference is removed.

- During GC, V8 gathers the JavaScript instance, and the splice is deallocated.

- The same Java instance is acquired a second time, and a new splice with a new JavaScript object is constructed and returned.

As a result, because the new instance can only obtain the Java properties of its matching native object, the property set to the initial JavaScript object is lost.

Splices Die Hard

Working with large, short-lived objects can easily result in out-of-memory crashes. Because of the Android splice's life cycle, disposing of large native instances necessitates a V8 GC followed by an Android VM GC (such as bitmaps).

Java Friendly

In general, the implementation is rather Java-friendly. It seldom necessitates the extra understanding of the runtime's inner workings.

Common Tips

Large native objects may survive longer than necessary due to the intrinsic memory management of objects in runtimes. This might occur if the JS garbage collector does not execute for an extended period after the object has become GC-eligible. As a consequence, this object will retain a strong reference on the native side.

One solution is to do several trash collections – both in JS/TS and on the native side (in case of running on Android). This is not, however, a low-cost business. Hand-triggering garbage pickups are not only time-consuming, but it may also interrupt routine garbage management.

Another solution is to use the releaseNativeCounterpart method, which takes an instance of a native class as an argument and removes its strong reference in the runtimes. By doing so, the Android native garbage collector can destroy the potentially hefty native object on its next run if it considers it dead. Because there is no trash collector on iOS, invoking this function reduces the reference count of the native object by one, and if there are no other uses for this object, it is removed.

If we try to utilize the native object in JS/TS after using the releaseNativeCounterpart function, the behavior is unclear, thus only use this function if we are certain the object will not be used again.

In JS/TS, here's an example of how to use the releaseNativeCounterpart function:

```
const heavyNativeObject = new com.native.HeavyObject();
releaseNativeCounterpart(heavyNativeObject); // All
heavyNativeObject usages following this line would
have unknown behavior
```

USER INTERFACE LAYOUT PROCESS

NativeScript has a recursive layout framework that allows you to scale and arrange views on the screen. The process of measuring and placing layout containers and their child views is known as layout. The layout is a time-consuming technique, with the number of children and the complexity of the layout container determining its speed and performance. A basic layout container, such as AbsoluteLayout, may outperform a more complicated layout container, such as GridLayout.

The layout is done in two passes: a measure pass and a layout pass. To that aim, each View has measurement and layout tools. Furthermore, each layout container has its onMeasure and onLayout methods for achieving its unique layout.

Measure Pass

Each View is measured during the measure pass to determine its target size. The measure pass evaluates the following qualities:

- height

- width

- visibility

- minWidth

- minHeight

- marginTop

- marginLeft

- marginBottom

- marginRight

Layout Pass

Each View is assigned to a single layout slot during the layout stage. The intended size of the view (as defined by the measure pass) and the following characteristics determine this slot:

- marginTop

- marginRight

- horizontalAlignment

- verticalAlignment

- marginLeft

- marginBottom

Layout Properties
Margins

The distance between view and its parent is described by the four margin attributes (marginRight, marginTop, marginLeft, and marginBottom).

When you set margins using XML, you have the option of using one of the following methods:

- **Set a single value:** Please provide a single value that will be applied to all sides of the view.

- **Set the following two values:** Provide two values. The first value is applied to the top-side, and the second to the right-side. The first value is then put to the bottom, while the second value is placed to the left-side (in that order).

- **Set the following four values:** Give each margin four values. The first value is applied to the top, the second to the right, the third to the bottom, and the fourth to the left.

Padding

The padding attributes (paddingRight, paddingTop, paddingLeft, and paddingBottom) define the space between the layout container and its children.

When you set paddings using XML, we can choose one of three techniques:

- **Set a single value:** Provide a single value applied to all sides of the view.

- **Set the following two values:** Provide two values. The first value is applied to the top side and the second to the right side. The first value is then put to the bottom, while the second value is placed on the left side (in that order).

- **Set the following four values:** For each padding, provide four values. The first value is applied to the top, the second value to the right, and the third value to the bottom, as well the fourth value to the left side (in that order).

Alignments

The layout uses horizontal and vertical alignment only when an element is given more space than it requires.

The following table lists the permissible horizontalAlignment values.

Member	Description
Left	The view is aligned to the left of parent element's layout slot.
Center	The view is aligned to the center of parent element's layout slot.
Right	The view is positioned to the right of the parent element's layout slot.
Stretch	The view is extended to fill the parent element's layout slot; if the width is specified, it takes priority.

The following table lists the permissible verticalAlignment values.

Member	Description
Top	The view is positioned at the top of the parent element's layout slot.
Centre	The view is aligned to the center of the parent element's layout slot.
Bottom	The view is positioned at the bottom of the parent element's layout slot.
Stretch	The view is extended to fill the parent element's layout slot; if height is specified, it takes priority.

Percentage Support

NativeScript allows us to provide % values for width, height, and margin. When a layout pass begins, the percent values are initially calculated based on the parent available size. This implies that if we position two buttons with height='50%' on a vertical StackLayout, they will take up the entire available height (e.g., they will fill the StackLayout vertically). The same holds true for margin characteristics. For example, if we specify margin-Left='5%', the element will have a margin equal to 5% of the parent's available width.

iOS Safe Area Support

The iOS Safe Area is a concept introduced by Apple in iOS 11. It is the screen region that is free to utilize and will not be impeded by system hardware or software. The safe zone does not always exist. It is influenced by the notch, the rounded edges of the screen, the status bar, the home indication, and elements of our program, such as the action bar and the tab bar. Refer to the Apple documentation for a better understanding.

NativeScript has included a default handling method for the iOS Safe Area since version 5.0. Certain container View components (those that can have children) overflow the safe area and are spread out to the screen's boundaries by default. These container components are as follows:

- Layouts

- ListView

- Repeater

- WebView

- ScrollView

The internal workflow is as follows:

- **Measure pass:** All components are measured in the screen's safe region.

- **Layout pass:** All components are displayed in full screen but are off-set to the safe area borders.

- **Layout pass:** If the component is close to the safe region, it is altered and enlarged to the screen's edges.

iosOverflowSafeArea Property

The default behavior described above should give decent UX right out of the box. Additionally, NativeScript 5.0 introduces the iosOverflowSafeArea property, which may be used to modify how components handle the iOS Safe Area. If we want the component to extend to the screen's boundaries when it borders the safe region, set this property value to true. To expressly avoid this behavior, set it to false. True is the default value for container components. All other components are considered content that should be limited to the safe region and is set to false by default.

Layout

LayoutBase is the root class for all views that enable child element placement.

Elements may be positioned using the various layout containers. They assess View's fundamental features, such as width, height, minWidth, and alignments, and reveal extra properties for arranging child views.

Predefined Layouts

The following table lists the default layouts provided by NativeScript.

Default Layouts Provided by NativeScript

Layouts	Description
[FlexboxLayout][FlexboxLayout]	This is a non-conforming CSS Flexible Box Layout implementation.
[AbsoluteLayout][AbsoluteLayout]	This layout allows us to specify the exact placement of its children (left/top coordinates).
[DockLayout][DockLayout]	This layout places its children on the outside edges and allows the last kid to take up the remaining space.
[GridLayout][GridLayout]	This layout specifies a rectangle layout area with columns and rows.
[StackLayout][StackLayout]	The children in this layout are arranged horizontally or vertically. The orientation attribute determines the direction.
[WrapLayout][WrapLayout]	Based on the orientation parameter, this layout arranges its children in rows or columns until the space is filled, then wraps them on a new row or column.

COMPONENTS

Action Bar

NativeScript's ActionBar is an abstraction of the Android ActionBar and iOS NavigationBar. It is a toolbar that appears at the top of the activity window and can include a title, application-level navigation, and other custom interactive objects.

Usage

The ActionBar has a title property and may be expanded with one or more ActionItem components and one NavigationButton.

```
<ActionBar title="ActionBar Title">
    <NavigationButton icon="res://ic_arrow_back_
black_24dp" (tap)="goBack()"></NavigationButton>
```

```
    <ActionItem icon="font://&#xf013;" class="fas" ios.
position="left" (tap)="openSettings()"></ActionItem>
</ActionBar>
```

ActionItem

For iOS and Android, the ActionItem components enable platform-specific position and systemIcon.

```
<ActionBar title="Action Items">
    <ActionItem (tap)="onShare()" ios.systemIcon="10"
ios.position="right"
                    android.systemIcon="ic_menu_share"
android.position="actionBar">
    </ActionItem>
    <ActionItem text="delete" (tap)="onDelete()"
                ios.systemIcon="15" ios.
position="left" android.position="popup">
    </ActionItem>
</ActionBar>
```

Android establishes position using android.position:

- **actionBar:** Inserts an item into the ActionBar. The action item might be shown as text or as an icon.

- **popup:** Displays the item's options menu. Items will be shown in text.

- **actionBarIfRoom:** It places the item in the ActionBar if there is space. Otherwise, it is added to the options menu.

iOS determines location using ios.position:

- **left:** Positions the item on the ActionBar's left side.

- **right:** Positions the item on the ActionBar's right side.

NavigationButton

The NavigationButton component is a generalization of the iOS back button and the Android navigation button.

- **iOS Specifications:** The navigation button's default text is the previous page's title. The back button is expressly used for navigating in iOS.

It navigates to the previous page, and we can't alter this behavior using the tap event. We may use ActionItem with ios.position="left" to add a button on the left side of the ActionBar and handle the tap event.

- **Android Specifics:** We cannot set text within the navigation button in Android. We may utilize the icon attribute to provide an image (e.g., ~\images\nav-image.png or res:ic_nav). We may use android.systemIcon to set one of the system icons available in Android. In this scenario, there is no default behavior for the NavigationButton tap event, and we must declare the callback code that will be called explicitly.

Styling

Only the background-color and color attributes may be used to customize the ActionBar. We could also use @nativescript/theme and utilize the default styles for each theme. Icon Fonts with the font://prefix can be used in the icon attribute of ActionItem. A new image will be created and assigned as an ActionItem's icon resource by specifying this prefix. We must supply the font size while utilizing this capability, which will compute the size of the output picture based on the device's dpi.

```
<!-- The default background-color and colour of
ActionBar and ActionItem are controlled by
nativescript-theme (if used) -->
<ActionBar title="Styling">
    <!-- Explicitly hiding the NavigationBar to
prevent the default one on iOS-->
    <NavigationButton visibility="collapsed">
</NavigationButton>

    <!-- Using icon property and Icon Fonts -->
    <ActionItem position="left"
icon="font://&#xf0a8;" class="fas" (tap)="goBack()">
</ActionItem>

    <!-- Creating custom views for the ActionItem-->
    <ActionItem ios.position="right">
        <GridLayout width="110">
            <Button text="Theme" class="-primary
-rounded-lg"></Button>
        </GridLayout>
    </ActionItem>
</ActionBar>
```

Properties
ActionBar Properties

Name	Type	Description
Title	string	Gets or sets the title of the action bar.
titleView	View	This method returns or sets the title view. When configured, a custom view replaces the title.

ActionItem Properties

Name	Type	Description
Text	string	Gets or sets the text of the action item.
Icon	string	Gets or sets the icon of the action item. Supports local images (~/), resources (res://), and icon fonts (fonts://).
ios.position	enum: "left", "right"	Sets the position of the item (default value is left).
android.position	enum: "actionBar", "popup", "actionBarIfRoom"	Sets the position of the item (default value is actionBar).
ios.systemIcon	number	iOS only: Sets the icon of the action item while using UIBarButtonSystemIcon enumeration.
android.systemIcon	string	Android only: Sets a path to a resource icon (see the list of Android system drawables).

NavigationButton Properties

Name	Type	Description
Text	string	Gets or sets the action item's text.
Icon	string	Gets or sets the action item's icon.

Events

Name	Description
Loaded	When the view is loaded, this event is emitted.
Unloaded	When the view is unloaded, this event is emitted.
layoutChanged	When the layout limits of a view change due to layout processing, this event is emitted.

API References

Name	Type
ActionBar	Module
ActionBar	Class
ActionItem	Class
ActionItems	Class
NavigationButton	Class

Animation

Adding animations to your application is one method to make it more appealing. NativeScript presents a simple and easy-to-use API that is strong enough to allow us to animate practically any native element in your application.

Animation Properties

We may use NativeScript to animate the properties of any element we desire. The properties will be animated after the animate method parameters (e.g., scale, rotate, duration, etc.) are specified.

The following NativeScript attributes can be animated: Opacity backgroundColor, translateX and translateY, scaleX and scaleY rotate the width and height.

In every animation, we can control the following properties:

- **duration:** The duration of the animation.

- **delay:** The length of time to wait before beginning the animation.

- **iterations:** The number of times the animation should be performed.

- **curve:** The animation's speed curve. The available alternatives are shown below.

Properties

Javascript Property	Value Description
backgroundColor	Accepts hex or Color value.
Curve	Timing function that uses the AnimationCurve enumeration.
Delay	Delay the animation started in milliseconds.
Duration	Duration of animation in milliseconds.

(Continued)

Javascript Property	Value Description
Iterations	The number of times to repeat animation.
Opacity	The number value (0–1 where 0 is full opacity).
Rotate	The number value for degrees (0–360 degrees).
Scale	Object value { x:1, y:2 } (1 = Original scale).
Translate	Object value { x:110, y:210 }.
Width	Value of number.
Height	Value of number.

Animating the opacity and background of a label is a basic example:

```
label.animate({
    opacity: 0.74,
    backgroundColor: new Color("Blue"),
    translate: { x: 210, y: 210 },
    scale: { x: 3, y: 3 },
    rotate: 180,
    duration: 2500,
    delay: 22,
    iterations: 5,
    curve: enums.AnimationCurve.easeIn
}).then(() => {
    console.log("Animation-finished");
}).catch((e) => {
    console.log(e.message);
});
```

Button

A Button component provides a simple means of interacting with the application and running custom code in response. When the user presses it, the button executes any associated actions.

Usage

The tap event of a Button component can be used to execute custom logic. It is as simple as using (tap) in HTML and adding a tap handler in our component to handle the event.

```
<Button text="Tap me!" (tap)="onTap($event)"></Button>
```

Styling

CSS or comparable attributes may be used to style the Button component.

```
<StackLayout>
    <!-- No styles applied -->
    <Button text="Button"></Button>
    <!-- Using local CSS class -->
    <Button text=".my-button" class="my-button">
</Button>
    <!-- Using @nativescript/theme CSS classes -->
    <Button text="Button.-primary" class="-primary">
</Button>
    <Button class="-primary">
        <FormattedString>
            <Span text="&#xf099;" class="fab"></Span>
            <Span text=" Button.-primary with icon">
</Span>
        </FormattedString>
    </Button>
    <Button text="Button.-outline" class="-outline">
</Button>
    <Button text="Button.-primary.-rounded-sm"
class="-primary -rounded-sm"></Button>
    <Button text="Button.-primary.-rounded-lg"
class="-primary -rounded-lg"></Button>
    <Button text="Button.-outline.-rounded-sm"
class="-outline -rounded-sm"></Button>
    <Button text="Button.-outline.-rounded-lg"
class="-outline -rounded-lg"></Button>
    <Button text="Button.-outline[isEnabled=false]"
isEnabled="false" class="-outline"></Button>
    <Button text="Button.-primary[isEnabled=false]"
isEnabled="false" class="-primary"></Button>
</StackLayout>
```

Specific Styling Properties

Name	CSS Name	Type	Description
androidElevation	android-elevation	Number	(Only for Android) The elevation of the android view may be retrieved or adjusted.
androidDynamic ElevationOffset	android-dynamic- elevation-offset	Number	(Only for Android) The dynamic elevation offs are obtained or set.

Gestures

Users may interact with our app by manipulating UI components on the screen using gestures, such as tap, slide, and pinch.

View, the foundation class for all NativeScript UI elements, contains on and off methods in NativeScript that allow us to subscribe or unsubscribe to any events and gestures detected by the UI element.

As the first argument, you specify whether the method should be turned on or off and the sort of gesture we wish to capture. The second argument is a function that is called each time the gesture supplied is recognized. If applicable, the function parameters include extra information about the gesture.

NativeScript gestures that are supported include:

- Tap

- Rotation

- Double Tap

- Long Press

- Touch

- Pan

- Pinch

- Swipe

Slider

The NativeScript Slider component allows the user to pick a value by dragging a control. Set the component's minValue and maxValue to specify the particular range to be used.

Usage

```
<Slider value="11" minValue="0" maxValue="90"
        (valueChange)="onSliderValueChange($event)">
</Slider>
```

Styling

```
<Slider value="9" minValue="0" maxValue="90"
        backgroundColor="green" color="blue">
</Slider>
```

Switch

The Switch component lets users switch between two states of a control. The component's default state is off or false, but we may modify it by changing the checked property to a boolean value. The checkedChange property, which informs the app when the value changes, may manage the state change event.

Usage

```
<Switch checked="true" (checkedChange)="onCheckedChange
($event)"></Switch>
```

Styling

The Swtich control's style characteristics are as follows:

- **color:** Sets the color of the handle.

- **backgroundColor (background-color in CSS):** Sets the color of the background when the switch is turned on.

  - **offBackgroundColor (off-background-color in CSS):** Sets the background color when the switch is turned off.

    ```
    <Switch color="blue" backgroundColor="yellow"
    offBackgroundColor="green">
    </Switch>
    ```

DatePicker

As a ready-to-use dialog, the DatePicker control allows the user to select a date. Each date portion – for day, month, and year – may be chosen independently by its relevant area of control.

Usage

Using DatePicker is as simple as setting the year, month, and day. We may also change the date property (accepts a Date object). We may also specify a minDate and a maxDate if necessary.

```
<DatePicker year="1990" month="5" day="23"
            [minDate]="minDate" [maxDate]="maxDate"
            (dateChange)="onDateChanged($event)"
            (dayChange)="onDayChanged($event)"
```

```
            (monthChange)="onMonthChanged($event)"
            (yearChange)="onYearChanged($event)"
            (loaded)="onDatePickerLoaded($event)"
            verticalAlignment="center">
</DatePicker>
```

Styling

```
.date-picker {
    background-color: olivedrab;
    border-color: lightgrey;
    border-width: 3;
    border-radius: 10;
    color: whitesmoke;
    vertical-align: middle;
}
```

Properties

Name	Type	Description
Date	Date	This method gets or sets the comple date as a Date object.
minDate	Date	gets or sets the minimum date.
maxDate	Date	Gets or sets the maximum date.
Day	number	Gets or sets the day, and the days start from 1.
Month	number	Gets or sets the month, and the months start from 1.
Year	number	Gets or sets year.

HtmlView

The HtmlView represents a view that contains HTML content. When we want to display static HTML content with base HTML support, use this component instead of a WebView.

Usage

```
<HtmlView [html]="htmlString" ></HtmlView>
```

Properties

Name	Type	Description
Html	string	This method returns or sets the HTML string. HTML support is limited; for more extensive support, try WebView.

TimePicker

As a ready-to-use dialog, NativeScript includes a TimePicker control that allows users to select a time. Each time component may be chosen independently by its appropriate control area for the hour, minutes, and AM/PM.

Usage

The TimePicker component may be defined by the hour and minute (numeric values only) or by defining the date attribute (accepts a Date object).

```
<TimePicker hour="8"
            minute="24"
            maxHour="22"
            maxMinute="57"
            minuteInterval="4"
            (timeChange)="onTimeChanged($event)">
</TimePicker>
```

Properties

Name	Type	Description
Hour	number	Gets or sets time hour.
maxHour	number	Gets or sets maximum time hour.
maxMinute	number	Gets or sets maximum time minute.
minHour	number	Gets or sets minimum time hour.
minMinute	number	Gets or sets minimum time minute.
Minute	number	Gets or sets time minute.
minuteInterval	number	Gets or sets time hour.
Time	Date	Gets or sets time while passing a Date object.

Tabs

The Tabs component allows us to easily switch between multiple views while maintaining a consistent user interface across iOS and Android devices. A mid-level navigation scenario is proposed for Tabs.

Roundup of Tabs components:

- **Semantic:** Navigation at the Mid-Level.

- **Usage:** We can have an unlimited number of tabs with the same purpose.

- **Transitions:** A slide transition that indicates their relative location to one another.

- Swipe Gesture is a gesture.

- **Preloading:** At least one to each side (because of the swipe gesture).

Usage

The Tabs component is divided into two sub-components:

- The bottom bar and its TabStripItem components are defined and rendered by the TabStrip.

- Multiple TabContentItem components, the total number of which should equal the number of tabs (TabStripItem components). Each TabContentItem serves as a container for the content of our tabs.

```
<Tabs selectedIndex="1">
    <!-- The bottom tab UI is created via TabStrip and
TabStripItem (for each tab)-->
    <TabStrip>
        <TabStripItem>
            <Label text="Home"></Label>
            <Image src="font://&#xf015;" class="fas">
</Image>
        </TabStripItem>
        <TabStripItem class="special">
            <Label text="Account's"></Label>
            <Image src="font://&#xf007;" class="fas">
</Image>
        </TabStripItem>
        <TabStripItem class="special">
            <Label text="Searchs"></Label>
            <Image src="font://&#xf00e;" class="fas">
</Image>
        </TabStripItem>
    </TabStrip>
    <!-- Number of TabContentItem components should
corespond to the number of TabStripItem components -->
    <TabContentItem>
        <GridLayout>
            <Label text="Home-Page" class="h2
text-center"></Label>
```

```
        </GridLayout>
    </TabContentItem>
    <TabContentItem>
        <GridLayout>
            <Label text="Account-Page" class="h2 text-
center"></Label>
        </GridLayout>
    </TabContentItem>
    <TabContentItem>
        <GridLayout>
            <Label text="Search-Page" class="h2 text-
center"></Label>
        </GridLayout>
    </TabContentItem>
</Tabs>
```

Styling

Three unique parameters that should be specified on the TabStrip component are used to introduce the significant style possibilities.

- **selectedItemnColor:** This property specifies the text color of the chosen tab strip item. When icon is an icon font (font://), it also changes
the color of the tab strip icon.

- **unSelectedItemColor:** Changes the text color of the tab strip items
that are not selected. When icon is an icon font (font://), it also
changes the color of the tab strip icon.

- **highlightColor:** This property determines the color of the underlin-
ing for the specified tab strip item.

These attributes can be changed dynamically, inline, or using CSS:

```
TabStrip {
    selected-item-color: blueviolet;
    un-selected-item-color: brown;
    highlight-color: brown;
}

TabContentItem.first-tabcontent {
    background-color: seashell;
    color: green;
```

```
}
TabContentItem.second-tabcontent {
    background-color: slategray;
    color: yellow;
}
TabContentItem.third-tabcontent {
    background-color: blueviolet;
    color: white;
}
```

WebView

The WebView component is used in our application to show web resources. We utilize the control by specifying src property that takes a URL, a path to a local HTML file, or an HTML string directly.

Usage

```
<WebView [src]="webViewSrc"
         (loadStarted)="onLoadStarted($event)"
         (loadFinished)="onLoadFinished($event)">
</WebView>
```

In the above code, we are configuring loadStarted and loadFinished events. When the source of the WebView component changes, both events are emitted (change the URL or load local HTML file). The loadStarted event is fired when the WebView source begins loading, and the loadFinished event is fired after the source is fully loaded. The events will produce data of the type LoadEventData.

Tips & Tricks

Gestures in WebView:

```
<GridLayout rows="52 52 *">
    <Label row="0" #touchlabel [text]="touchResult"
textWrap="true" ></Label>
    <Label row="1" #panlabel [text]="panResult"
textWrap="true" ></Label>
    <WebView row="2" (loaded)="onWebViewLoaded($ev
ent)"  (touch)="webViewTouch($event)" (pan)=
"webViewPan($event)" [src]="webViewSrc" ></WebView>
</GridLayout>
```

USER INTERFACE STYLING

In a NativeScript application, we alter the looks and appearance of views (elements) in the same way we do in a web application, either using Cascading Style Sheets (CSS) or by modifying the style object of the components in JavaScript. CSS language support is limited to a subset of the CSS language.

Similar to the DOM Style Object, each View instance provides a style property that contains all of the view's style attributes. All of the view's style attributes are applied to the underlying native widget when it is presented.

Applying CSS Styles

CSS styles may be applied at three distinct levels:

- CSS that applies to all application pages is known as application-wide CSS.

- **Component-specific CSS:** This only applies to components.

- **Inline CSS:** CSS that is applied straight to a UI view.

If CSS is defined at many levels, all of them will be applied. The inline CSS will be prioritized, whereas the application CSS will be prioritized last.

Platform-specific CSS can also be used.

Application-Wide CSS

NativeScript checks if the file app.css exists when the program starts. If it does, any CSS styles contained in it are loaded and applied to all application pages. This file is a handy place to keep styles that will be used on several pages.

The name of the file from which the application-wide CSS is loaded can be changed. We must modify before starting the program, often in the app.js or app.ts file, as seen below:

```
platformNativeScriptDynamic({
bootInExistingPage:false, cssFile:"style.css" });
```

Component-Specific CSS

Because everything in an Angular application is a component, it is a fairly typical task to add some CSS code that should only apply to one component. Using a component's styles or styleUrls property to add component-specific CSS to a NativeScript-Angular app.

```
@Component({
    selector: 'list-test',
    styles: ['.third { background-color: yellow; }'],
    template:. .
```

The CSS rules in each of these instances will only apply to the stated component and not to other UI components in the application.

Adding CSS String

This snippet adds a new style to the existing collection. This is quite handy when we need to add a small CSS chunk to an element (for testing reasons, for example):

```
page.addCss("button {background-color: yellow}");
```

Adding CSS File

This code snippet adds additional CSS styles to the existing collection. This approach, on the other hand, reads them from a file. It may be used to organize styles in files and reuse them across numerous pages.

```
page.addCssFile(cssFileName);
```

Inline CSS

CSS, like HTML, may be specified inline in the XML markup for a UI view:

```
<Button text="inline style" style="background-color:
yellow;"></Button>
```

Platform-Specific CSS

NativeScript principles make it simple to use platform-specific CSS, either through separate style sheets or in-line declarations. This page in the documentation provides an overview of NativeScript's convention-based file naming conventions for aiming files at various platforms and screen sizes.

Note: When using Angular, filename rules do not function to target specific screen sizes or orientations. To the runtime, JavaScript is necessary to target styles at various displays. See this post for an example of Angular aiming styles toward tablets.

There are four basic methods for targeting styles on iOS or Android:

- Platform specific style sheets (styles.component.ios.css, styles. component.android.css)

- Platform specific markup blocks (<ios> ... </ios>, <android> ... </android>)

- Platform specific attributes (<Label ios:style="..." android:style="...")

- Platform specific CSS rules (:host-content(.ns-ios) .mystyle { ... }, :host-context(.ns-android) .mystyle { ... })

Multiple style sheets and CSS imports are the most frequent and stable techniques for handling platform-agnostic and platform-specific styles in NativeScript. To see this pattern in action, try out this Playground example.

Using this pattern, a page (or component) contains three different style sheets: common, iOS, and Android. For example, for the page home.component.html, there would be three style sheets:

- home-common.css

- home.component.ios.css

- home.component.android.css

Supported Selectors

NativeScript recognizes a subset of CSS selector syntax. Here's how to utilize the selectors that are supported:

- Class selector

- Type selector

- Hierarchical selector

- ID selector

- Pseudo selector

- Attribute selector

Type Selector

Type selectors in NativeScript, like CSS element selectors, select all views of a specified type. Because type selectors are not case sensitive, we may use both button and Button.

```
button { background-color: yellow }
```

Class Selector

Class selectors choose all views that belong to a specific class. The class is specified using the view's className attribute.

Note: To add a class to an element in JS/TS, the class rule must be in a CSS file higher up the component tree than the element, such as app.css.

```
.title { font-size: 30 }
```

ID Selector

Id selectors pick all views that have the same id. The view's id is set using the id attribute.

```
#login-button { background-color: grey }
```

Hierarchical Selector

A CSS selector may contain more than one basic selector, and a combinatory symbol may be added between selectors.

- Descendant selection (space). For example, the following code will pick all buttons within StackLayouts.

```
StackLayout Button { background-color: blue; }
```

- (>) – A selection for direct children. Using the preceding example, if the CSS is modified to:

```
StackLayout > Button { background-color: blue; }
```

  The background-color regulation is not going to be enforced. To use the selector, the WrapLayout element must be deleted so that the Button becomes a direct child of the StackLayout.

- (+) – An adjacent sibling selector allows us to choose all elements that are siblings to a given element.

Classified Direct Sibling Test:

```
<StackLayout class="layout-class">
    <Label text="Direct sibling test by id"></Label>
    <Button class="test-child" text="FirstButton">
</Button>
    <Button class="test-child-2"
text="SecondButton"></Button>
</StackLayout>
```

Classified Direct Sibling ID:

```
<StackLayout class="layout-class">
    <Label text="Direct sibling test by id"></Label>
    <Button id="test-child" text="FirstButton">
</Button>
    <Button id="test-child-2" text="SecondButton">
</Button>
</StackLayout>
```

Classified Direct Sibling Type:

```
<StackLayout class="direct-sibling--type">
    <Label text="Direct sibling by type"></Label>
    <Button text="TestButton"></Button>
    <Label text="TestLabel"></Label>
    <Button text="TestButton"></Button>
    <Label text="TestLabel"></Label>
    <Button text="TestButton"></Button>
    <Label text="TestLabel"></Label>
</StackLayout>
```

Attribute Selector

```
button[testAttr]{ background-color: green; }
```

This selector will pick all buttons that have the testAttr attribute set to some value.

Some more sophisticated situations are also supported:

- **button[testAttr='flower']** {...}: CSS will be applied to all buttons with the testAttr attribute set to the value flower.

- **button[testAttr˜='flower'] {...}:** All buttons having a testAttr attribute containing a space-separated list of words, one of which is "flower," are selected.

- **button[testAttr|='flower'] {...}:** Selects all buttons with a testAttr property value that starts with "flower." The value has to be a whole word, either alone like btn['testAttr'] = 'flower', or followed by hyphen (-), like btn['testAttr'] = 'flower-house'.

- **button[testAttr^='flower'] {...}:** All buttons having a testAttr attribute value that starts with "flower" are selected. It is not necessary for the value to be a whole word.

- **button[testAttr$='flower'] {...}:** All buttons having a testAttr attribute value that ends in "flower" are selected. It is not necessary for the value to be a whole word.

- **button[testAttr*='flo'] {...}:** All buttons having a testAttr attribute value of "flo" are selected. It is not necessary for the value to be a whole word.

Attribute selectors could be used alone or could be combined with all type of CSS selectors.

```
#login-button[testAttr='flower'] { background-color:
white; }
[testAttr] {color: yellow;}
```

Pseudo Selector
A pseudo selector, also known as a pseudo class, is used to specify an element's specific state. NativeScript currently only supports the highlighted pseudo selector.

Root Views CSS Classes   NativeScript adds a CSS class to the application's root views for particular states to enable flexible style and theme.
The following are the default CSS classes:

- **.ns-root:** class that is associated with the application's root view.

- **.ns-modal:** class that is associated with the modal root view.

CSS classes for each application and modal root view are as follows:

- .ns-android and .ns-ios are classes that define the application platform.

- .ns-phone and .ns-tablet are device-specific classes.

- .ns-portrait, .ns-landscape, and .ns-unknown classes that define the application orientation.

- .ns-light and .ns-dark are classes that define the look of the system.

BASICS OF THE NativeScript COMMAND-LINE INTERFACE

In this section, we'll learn the fundamentals of the NativeScript command-line interface, such as creating new applications, getting those apps running on devices, and setting up a development pipeline that allows us to iterate quickly.

Developing Applications

The NativeScript CLI is used to develop and run programs in NativeScript. After installation, the NativeScript CLI is available as a tns command (Telerik NativeScript) on our terminal or command prompt.

In this part, we will become acquainted with the NativeScript CLI and use the CLI's create command to launch our first NativeScript app.

Try with the tns create command.

To build a new NativeScript application, open our terminal or command prompt and type the following command:

```
tns create HelloEveryone --template
tns-template-blank-ng
```

We're telling the NativeScript CLI to build an app using a predetermined template named "tns-template-blank-ng" by supplying two arguments to the create command: HelloEveryone, which specifies the app's name we're constructing, and the template option.

Because the NativeScript CLI needs to download a few dependencies while setting up our new project, the create command will take a minute to finish.

When the program completes, use the cd command (change directory) to go to our new app folder.

```
cd HelloEveryone
```

Running Applications

Once our NativeScript mobile project has been established, we have two options for starting the application:

- Using the preview command to run a preview build. This option allows us to test NativeScript quickly.

- Using the run command to perform a local build. This option provides us with the complete development experience (building and deploying on local emulators and devices).

Using PREVIEW Quick Setup

Now that we've scaffolded an app on our local computer, we're ready to execute it on a device.

Use tns Preview Command

We're working locally to the NativeScript Playground app for our iOS or Android device to link the app, so use the CLI's tns preview command. Let's have a look at how it works.

In our terminal or command prompt, type the following command:

```
tns preview
```

- In your terminal, we'll notice a QR code.

- Then, on your iOS or Android smartphone, launch the NativeScript Playground app.

- Scan the QR code that displays in our terminal or commands prompt using the Scan QR code option in the Playground app.

- After scanning, our app should appear on our smartphone.

- Now that we've installed the program, we could discover that the tns preview command in your terminal or command prompt never completed. That is, we are unable to type on our terminal.

This is because the tns preview command is now monitoring our project for updates. When the tns preview command detects a code change, it automatically refreshes or livesyncs our app so we can see the changes right away.

In this chapter, we covered Android emulator tips and how to create UI controls. We also covered custom webpack configuration and styling in NativeScript. Moreover, we learned about NativeScript conventions.

Appraisal

NativeScript is a well-known framework for front-end, cross-platform programming that creates genuinely native apps with JavaScript.

Progress created it in 2014, and it was rated "visionary" in Gartner's Magic Quadrant for Mobile App Dev Platforms (MADP).

It provides direct access to all native platform APIs using JavaScript, TypeScript, or Angular, resulting in enhanced native-like experiences on the web, iOS, and Android.

NativeScript is a free and open-source mobile app development framework for iOS and Android. It's a framework that was JIT-compiled. The JS virtual machine runs NativeScript code. On Android and iOS platforms, it makes use of the V8 engine runtime.

NativeScript helps developers create native, cross-platform programs quickly and efficiently while saving money on the development, testing, and training. As a result, native apps will remain rich and powerful for many years to come, making them better and easier to use.

NativeScript apps, as seen, are written in a combination of JavaScript, XML, and CSS.

Advantages of NativeScript:

- Simple learning curve

- Supported by a solid community

- Completely native performance

- One code, many platforms

- Direct, unrestricted access to iOS and Android APIs

- JavaScript, TypeScript, Angular, Vue, and CSS are all well supported

- A large number of plugins and templates are available to help with development speed

DOI: 10.1201/9781003299394-6

NativeScript is popular among developers and companies because of its use of XML for platform-independent user interfaces (UIs), Angular and Vue.js integration, code reusability, and native speed.

NativeScript-powered apps include Triodos Bank, Daily Nanny, Sennheiser, MyPUMA, Portable North Pole, and SAP.

Limitations of NativeScript:

- Apps take up more space than native apps.

- Plugins are required.

- An app is currently being debugged.

WHAT IS THE SIGNIFICANCE OF NativeScript?

NativeScript varies from other mobile app frameworks in various areas, aside from JIT compilation. The most important difference, we feel, is our ability to create native apps from a single code base and publish them unaltered to both Android and iOS.

We've worked with several mobile app frameworks in the past, and NativeScript stands out in our opinion.

QUICKLY REACHING THE MARKET

Write once, deploy everywhere, and so on. We don't want to waste your time, whether we're a company, a single developer, or a casual hobbyist. We'll also have more time to develop and provide more features in less time because we'll spend less time constructing a complete app.

WHAT ARE THE CAREER PROSPECTS IN NativeScript?

- NativeScript Developer

- Software Engineer – NativeScript Platform – Mobile Applications

- Angular with Nativescript (Mobile Application Developer)

- Nativescript App Developer

- Mobile Application Developer (Native script)

NativeScript outperforms React Native in three crucial ways:

- It is intended to be written once and run anywhere. React Native continues to necessitate platform-specific programming.

- Angular 2 is more user-friendly than React. It's simple to use Angular. React is difficult. Angular 2 (which has first-class support in NativeScript) seems to be even simpler than Angular 1.

- In NativeScript, we can write directly to native APIs from JavaScript (we don't need to develop a native plug-in to access a native API).

REACT Native VS. NativeScript: HOW TO SELECT THE BEST FRAMEWORK

While app growth and expansion have been ongoing in recent years, cross-platform mobile apps, for better or worse, are altering the commercial environment of every industry. As a result, the technological stack should be chosen as well. Let's look at the two lists that will assist us in creating the structure for developing our app concept.

NativeScript is the ideal option for programs that will be required to use JS or TypeScript:

- combines common iOS and Android capabilities

- where we will access web components using Angular or Vue

- jsweb application

With React Native, we'll remain ahead of the competition if our app:

- It has native-like performance on Android and iOS.

- In addition to Kotlin/Java and Objective-C/Swift, its codebase will feature UI components.

- It will be able to access hardware functions without the use of third-party extensions.

- The MVP is scheduled to be available in 3–4 weeks.

WHO IS MAKING USE OF NativeScript?

MyPumma, Raiffeisenbank, California Court Access App, Dockbooking, Regelneef, Daily Nanny, GeoAgro, BitPoints Wallet, and many more are among the NativeScript apps on display.

The framework shares the issue and goal knowledge of companies in the following industries:

- retail and shopping

- banking

- education

- government services

- booking services

- agriculture

- communication

- lifestyle

SIX THINGS WE SHOULD KNOW BEFORE LEARNING NativeScript

Javascript (TypeScript as Well)

Because NativeScript is a JavaScript framework, the first thing we'll need to learn is JavaScript. We also recommend studying TypeScript, which should be simple to understand if we already know JavaScript.

Although we can create NativeScript Core and NativeScript Vue applications using plain JavaScript, understanding TypeScript may be advantageous in the job market because more and more firms are incorporating it into their development workflow.

TypeScript is a JavaScript superset that adds optional static typing to the language. It features excellent tools that are beneficial both when working in a team and on big projects.

It features a strict structure that allows developers to produce less buggy code while also making it easier to comprehend.

If a junior developer joins a TypeScript-using organization, we will find it easier to comprehend and follow the codebase.

Because Angular utilizes TypeScript by default, NativeScript Angular does as well. If we're working on a NativeScript Angular application, we can't avoid learning TypeScript because NativeScript Angular doesn't allow us to create in plain JavaScript.

We may use either ordinary JavaScript or TypeScript with NativeScript Core and NativeScript Vue.

UI Layouts

The second thing we'll need to be familiar with is UI layouts. We're not talking about NativeScript-specific layouts here. What we mean is that we will need to be conversant with the layout of a UI. For example, suppose we're from the web. In that case, we're probably aware of the box model, which states that a UI may be divided into rectangles that include other rectangles and other items such as text and images. We'd also be familiar with layering – not only can we have rectangles next to each other in a 3D world, but we can also have rectangles on top of each other, so we won't only be dealing with x and y coordinates, but occasionally we'll also be dealing with the Z index.

We should apply this understanding to NativeScript since there are parallels between setting up DOM components and NativeScript Views. We may also render our rectangles in NativeScript to contain additional rectangles and items (in NativeScript, we call these Views because they inherit from the root View class). In a 3D environment, we may also stack our Views on top of one another.

We must be familiar with UI layouts. When we are given a design document for an app, we can dismantle it and know which individual widgets to utilize when constructing the NativeScript app.

User Experience

The third concept we should be acquainted with is User Experience (UX).

NativeScript enables us to create a single code base for both iOS and Android apps. As a result, we may wind up launching an app for both platforms that appears and functions identically on both. This may be OK for certain apps, but it may not be perfect for others.

While certain things are the same on iOS and Android, other UI design patterns are unique to that platform, and users of that platform will be accustomed to how the UI is set out and performs on that platform.

We should be familiar with the many UI design patterns that are suggested for both platforms. Both platforms include design rules that we should know while developing our app: the Human Interface Guidelines for iOS and the Material Design Guidelines for Android.

The beauty of NativeScript is that we can retain a single code base for both iOS and Android apps, sharing code between them while having the flexibility of adding different platform-specific code for each.

Software Design Patterns

Another point to remember relates to Software Design Patterns.

Before we begin coding, we should have a plan for structuring the code, the many components that will comprise our app, and how each component will interact with others.

Different Software Design Patterns are often used to structure code. For example, in NativeScript Core, the Model View ViewModel (MVVM) paradigm is extensively employed. MVVM allows us to divide our code into distinct concerns. The Model represents the app's data and business logic. The ViewModel is located between the Model and the View and serves as a conduit for information between the two. When there is a change in the Model, the ViewModel notifies the View so that the View may update itself appropriately.

It can also communicate events from the View to the Model. The View is in charge of the app's UI. It subscribes to the ViewModel to receive data and change UI components accordingly.

The Model View Controller (MVC) paradigm is used by default in NativeScript Angular and NativeScript Vue. The Controller is in terms of maintaining the Model and View up to date. It receives input and updates the associated variables. It communicates data between the Model and the View.

Core Modules

When studying NativeScript, we should also be well familiar with the framework's Core Modules.

NativeScript has several modules that are automatically packaged into your application when we create a new project. The Core Modules offer the necessary abstraction for accessing the underlying native platforms. The Gesture module, for example, exposes a standard JS API for translating application TypeScript/JavaScript code into native gestures API calls. The Core Modules also include a simple XML-based method for designing UIs, data binding, and navigation.

Core Modules have available modules that aid in the creation of our app's UI. For example, the layouts module under tns-core-modules offers layouts such as the StackLayout that assist us in arranging our UI elements.

UI components such as Buttons and Labels may also be found in tns-core-modules. Core Modules additionally provide networking, timing, application settings, and data features such as working with observables and observable arrays.

Learning Partners

We could learn NativeScript independently, but it's typically best to work with a Learning Partner. A Learning Partner can hold us accountable and keep us disciplined as we go through the learning process. Having someone to explain what we've just learned may help absorb things faster, and they can correct us when we're incorrect while also sharing their expertise. We may also collaborate on projects, sharing the amount of effort necessary to create a comprehensive app.

Bibliography

7 Things to Know When Learning NativeScript | NativeScripting. (n.d.). 7 Things to Know When Learning NativeScript | NativeScripting; nativescripting.com. Retrieved July 11, 2022, from https://nativescripting.com/posts/7-things-to-know-when-learning-nativescript

8 Steps to Publish Your NativeScript App to the App Stores | The NativeScript Blog. (n.d.). 8 Steps to Publish Your NativeScript App to the App Stores | The NativeScript Blog; blog.nativescript.org. Retrieved July 11, 2022, from https://blog.nativescript.org/steps-to-publish-your-nativescript-app-to-the-app-stores/

Ancheta, W. (2016, August 5). *Create Your First NativeScript App.* Code Envato Tuts+; code.tutsplus.com. https://code.tutsplus.com/tutorials/create-your-first-nativescript-app--cms-26957

Ancheta, W. (2016, August 5). *Create Your First NativeScript App.* Code Envato Tuts+; code.tutsplus.com. https://code.tutsplus.com/tutorials/create-your-first-nativescript-app--cms-26957

Ancheta, W. (2016, July 15). *An Introduction to NativeScript.* Code Envato Tuts+; code.tutsplus.com. https://code.tutsplus.com/articles/an-introduction-to-nativescript--cms-26771

Angular Tutorial | NativeScript. (n.d.). Angular Tutorial | NativeScript; docs.nativescript.org. Retrieved July 11, 2022, from https://docs.nativescript.org/tutorial/angular.html#create-a-new-nativescript-angular-application

Angular Tutorial | NativeScript. (n.d.). Angular Tutorial | NativeScript; docs.nativescript.org. Retrieved July 11, 2022, from https://docs.nativescript.org/tutorial/angular.html

Build web and mobile apps with Angular and NativeScript. (n.d.). Build Web and Mobile Apps with Angular and NativeScript; school.geekwall.in. Retrieved July 11, 2022, from https://school.geekwall.in/p/B1uK7M6LQ

CLI Basics – NativeScript Docs. (n.d.). CLI Basics – NativeScript Docs; v6.docs.nativescript.org. Retrieved July 11, 2022, from https://v6.docs.nativescript.org/angular/start/cli-basics

Components – NativeScript Docs. (n.d.). Components – NativeScript Docs; v7.docs.nativescript.org. Retrieved July 11, 2022, from https://v7.docs.nativescript.org/ui/overview

Creating a mobile app in NativeScript (Pt 1). (2019, July 26). Creating a Mobile App in NativeScript (Pt 1); www.merixstudio.com. https://www.merixstudio .com/blog/creating-mobile-app-nativescript-pt-1/

Data Binding – NativeScript Docs. (n.d.). Data Binding – NativeScript Docs; v7.docs.nativescript.org. Retrieved July 11, 2022, from https://v7.docs .nativescript.org/core-concepts/data-binding

Data binding · nativescript-batch. (n.d.). Nativescript-Batch; nativescript-batch. readme.io. Retrieved July 11, 2022, from https://nativescript-batch.readme. io/docs/data-binding

Develop iOS Apps on Windows With NativeScript Sidekick – DZone Mobile. (n.d.). Dzone.Com; dzone.com. Retrieved July 11, 2022, from https://dzone .com/articles/develop-ios-apps-on-windows-with-nativescript-side

Develop iOS Apps on Windows with NativeScript Sidekick | The NativeScript Blog. (n.d.). Develop iOS Apps on Windows with NativeScript Sidekick | The NativeScript Blog; blog.nativescript.org. Retrieved July 11, 2022, from https:// blog.nativescript.org/develop-ios-apps-on-windows-with-nativescript-sidekick/

EDUCBA. (n.d.). Introduction to NativeScript Layouts. Retrieved July 11, 2022, from https://www.educba.com/nativescript-layouts/

Environment Setup | NativeScript. (n.d.). Environment Setup | NativeScript; docs. nativescript.org. Retrieved July 11, 2022, from https://docs.nativescript.org/ environment-setup

EPS Software Corp., Nic Raboy, C. M. (n.d.). *NativeScript, iOS, Android – An Introduction to Native Android and iOS Development with NativeScript*. NativeScript, iOS, Android – An Introduction to Native Android and iOS Development with NativeScript; www.codemag.com. Retrieved July 11, 2022, from https://www.codemag.com/article/1711051/An-Introduction-to-Native-Android-and-iOS-Development-with-NativeScript

Gutta, S. (2015, August 28). *What is: Javascript Frameworks – An Introduction*. Atlantic. Net; www.atlantic.net. https://www.atlantic.net/vps-hosting/what-is-javascript-frameworks-introduction/

https://www.trustradius.com/products/nativescript/reviews#:~:text=It's%20 a%20great%20place%20to,the%20internet%20to%20get%20started.

INDIA, S. (2019, October 31). *What Is NativeScript? Quick Overview In 200 Words | by SPEC INDIA | Tech in 200 Words | Medium*. Medium; medium. com. https://medium.com/tech-in-200-words/what-is-nativescript-quick-overview-in-200-words-aa79dea932bc

iOS App Extensions – NativeScript Docs. (n.d.). iOS App Extensions – NativeScript Docs; v7.docs.nativescript.org. Retrieved July 11, 2022, from https://v7.docs. nativescript.org/tooling/ios-app-extensions#:~:text=iOS%20App%20 extensions%20give%20users,without%20having%20to%20open%20it

Layout Process – NativeScript Docs. (n.d.). Layout Process – NativeScript Docs; v6.docs.nativescript.org. Retrieved July 11, 2022, from https://v6.docs .nativescript.org/ui/layouts/layouts

Layouts – NativeScript Docs. (n.d.). Layouts – NativeScript Docs; v7.docs .nativescript.org. Retrieved July 11, 2022, from https://v7.docs.nativescript. org/angular/ui/ng-components/layouts

Layouts – NativeScript Docs. (n.d.). Layouts – NativeScript Docs; v7.docs.nativescript.org. Retrieved July 11, 2022, from https://v7.docs.nativescript.org/angular/ui/ng-components/layouts

Matviichuk, M. (2021, February 25). *NativeScript vs React Native: Choosing a Cross-Platform Framework | by Mariia Matviichuk | React Native Hub | Medium.* Medium; medium.com. https://medium.com/react-native-hub/nativescript-vs-react-native-choosing-a-cross-platform-framework-be066e928687#:~:text=NativeScript%20would%20be%20the%20best,you%20drop%20us%20a%20line

Metadata – NativeScript Docs. (n.d.). Metadata – NativeScript Docs; v6.docs.nativescript.org. Retrieved July 11, 2022, from https://v6.docs.nativescript.org/core-concepts/metadata

Modules – NativeScript Docs. (n.d.). Modules – NativeScript Docs; v7.docs.nativescript.org. Retrieved July 11, 2022, from https://v7.docs.nativescript.org/core-concepts/android-runtime/getting-started/modules

NativeScript – Architecture. (n.d.). NativeScript – Architecture; www.tutorialspoint.com. Retrieved July 11, 2022, from https://www.tutorialspoint.com/nativescript/nativescript_architecture.htm#:~:text=NativeScript%20is%20an%20advanced%20framework,optimized%20and%20advanced%20mobile%20application

NativeScript – Data Binding. (n.d.). NativeScript – Data Binding; www.tutorialspoint.com. Retrieved July 11, 2022, from https://www.tutorialspoint.com/nativescript/nativescript_data_binding.htm#:~:text=Data%20binding%20is%20one%20of,model%20without%20any%20programming%20effort

NativeScript – Installation. (n.d.). NativeScript – Installation; www.tutorialspoint.com. Retrieved July 11, 2022, from https://www.tutorialspoint.com/nativescript/nativescript_installation.htm

NativeScript – Modules. (n.d.). NativeScript – Modules; www.tutorialspoint.com. Retrieved July 11, 2022, from https://www.tutorialspoint.com/nativescript/nativescript_modules.htm

NativeScript – Native APIs Using JavaScript. (n.d.). NativeScript – Native APIs Using JavaScript; www.tutorialspoint.com. Retrieved July 11, 2022, from https://www.tutorialspoint.com/nativescript/nativescript_native_apis_using_javascript.htm

NativeScript – Navigation. (n.d.). NativeScript – Navigation; www.tutorialspoint.com. Retrieved July 11, 2022, from https://www.tutorialspoint.com/nativescript/nativescript_navigation.htm

NativeScript – Navigation. (n.d.). NativeScript – Navigation; www.tutorialspoint.com. Retrieved July 11, 2022, from https://www.tutorialspoint.com/nativescript/nativescript_navigation.htm#:~:text=Navigation%20enables%20users%20to%20quickly,clicks%20to%20more%20complex%20patterns

nativescript Tutorial – Accessing native apis. (n.d.). Nativescript Tutorial – Accessing Native Apis; sodocumentation.net. Retrieved July 11, 2022, from https://sodocumentation.net/nativescript/topic/5188/accessing-native-apis

nativescript Tutorial => Getting started with nativescript. (n.d.). Nativescript Tutorial => Getting Started with Nativescript; riptutorial.com. Retrieved July 11, 2022, from https://riptutorial.com/nativescript

NativeScript Tutorial. (n.d.). NativeScript Tutorial; www.tutorialspoint.com. Retrieved July 11, 2022, from https://www.tutorialspoint.com/nativescript/index.htm

NativeScript UI is Now Free—Here's How to Get Started | The NativeScript Blog. (n.d.). NativeScript UI Is Now Free—Here's How to Get Started | The NativeScript Blog; blog.nativescript.org. Retrieved July 11, 2022, from https://blog.nativescript.org/nativescript-ui-is-now-free-here-s-how-to-get-started/#:~:text=That%20means%20you%20can%20use,without%20 signing%20up%20for%20anything

Navigation – NativeScript Docs. (n.d.). Navigation – NativeScript Docs; v7.docs. nativescript.org. Retrieved July 11, 2022, from https://v7.docs.nativescript. org/core-concepts/angular-navigation

Patoliya, S. (2018, July 19). *How to Build Nativescript Angular ToDo Mobile App in 8 Steps | Blogs.* Blogs; www.teclogiq.com. https://www.teclogiq.com/blog/ nativescript-todo-application/

Removing Short Imports in NativeScript, the Easy Way (with VS Code) – DEV Community. (2019, July 17). DEV Community; dev.to. https://dev.to/toddanglin/ removing-short-imports-in-nativescript-the-easy-way-with-vs-code-660

Setting Up Android Emulators for NativeScript Development | Johannes' Blog. (n.d.). Setting Up Android Emulators for NativeScript Development | Johannes' Blog; blog.johanneshoppe.de. Retrieved July 11, 2022, from https://blog.johanneshoppe.de/2016/06/setting-up-android-emulators-for-nativescript-development/

Setup Android Emulators – NativeScript Docs. (n.d.). Setup Android Emulators – NativeScript Docs; v7.docs.nativescript.org. Retrieved July 11, 2022, from https://v7.docs.nativescript.org/tooling/android-virtual-devices

TekTutorialsHub. (2018, August 11). *Nativescript HelloWorld Example App with Angular – TekTutorialsHub.* TekTutorialsHub; www.tektutorialshub.com. https://www.tektutorialshub.com/nativescript/nativescript-helloworld-example-app-with-angular/

Tudip. (2020, July 16). *Create NativeScript App with Angular | Tudip Technologies.* Tudip; tudip.com. https://tudip.com/blog-post/create-nativescript-app-with-angular/

UI & Styling | NativeScript. (n.d.). UI & Styling | NativeScript; docs.nativescript. org. Retrieved July 11, 2022, from https://docs.nativescript.org/ui-and-styling.html

What Is a JavaScript Framework? – Skillcrush. (2018, July 23). Skillcrush; skillcrush. com. https://skillcrush.com/blog/what-is-a-javascript-framework/#:~:text= At%20their%20most%20basic%2C%20JS,websites%20or%20web%20 applications%20around

Why Choose NativeScript for AngularJS Mobile App Development? (n.d.). Radixweb; radixweb.com. Retrieved July 11, 2022, from https://radixweb. com/blog/angularjs-mobile-app-development-using-nativescript

Working with Data in NativeScript | The NativeScript Blog. (n.d.). Working with Data in NativeScript | The NativeScript Blog; blog.nativescript.org. Retrieved July 11, 2022, from https://blog.nativescript.org/working-with-data-in-nativescript/

Index